Yaru!

('Hello!')

This book is dedicated to my big brother the late Alan Santo (Tony), David Alley (Banggaru), Harold Alley (Wadhabara), Val Alberts, Eva Kennedy, the late Helen Bushman, my big sister Lillian (Santo) Daveys, Alan Huen, Billy Coleman, Gloria and Alex Santo, Richard Davidson (Dickie), Sadie McLane, Elsie Thompson, Irene Howe and Randel Ross and all the Gudjal people that have passed on.

—William Santo

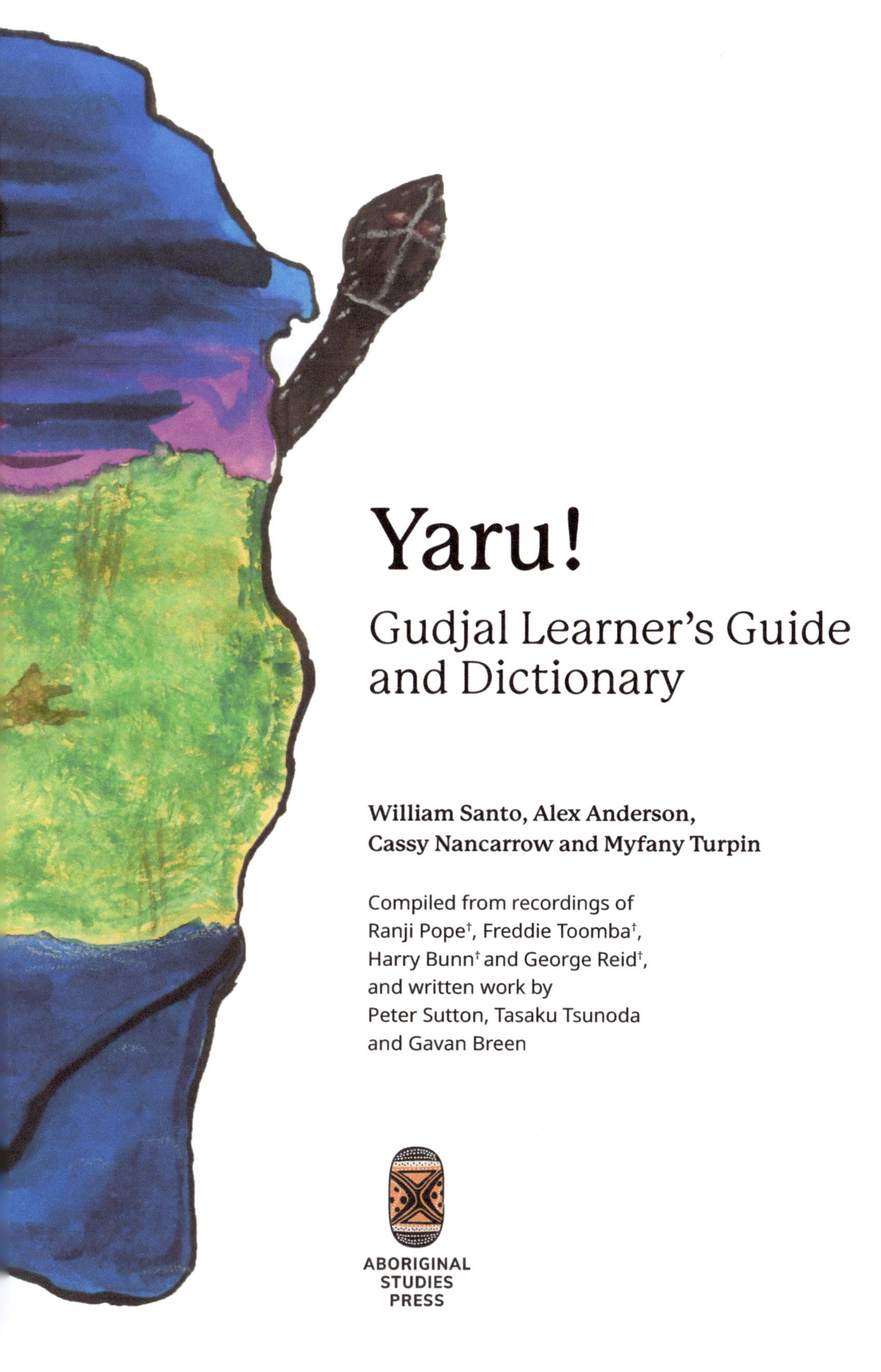

Yaru!

Gudjal Learner's Guide and Dictionary

**William Santo, Alex Anderson,
Cassy Nancarrow and Myfany Turpin**

Compiled from recordings of
Ranji Pope†, Freddie Toomba†,
Harry Bunn† and George Reid†,
and written work by
Peter Sutton, Tasaku Tsunoda
and Gavan Breen

ABORIGINAL
STUDIES
PRESS

First published in 2023
by Aboriginal Studies Press

Reprinted in 2026

Aboriginal and Torres Strait Islander people are respectfully advised that this publication contains names and images of deceased persons and culturally sensitive information.

Aboriginal Studies Press is the publishing arm of the Australian Institute of Aboriginal and Torres Strait Islander Studies.

GPO Box 553, Canberra, ACT 2601
Phone: (61 2) 6246 1183
Fax: (61 2) 6261 4288
Email: asp@aiatsis.gov.au
Web: www.aiatsis.gov.au/asp/about.html

The full audio for this book can be downloaded here.

A catalogue record for this work is available from the National Library of Australia

ISBN: 978-1-922102-44-7 (pb);
978-1-922102-74-4 (ebook)

Cover image: *Mural (Charters Towers) and Gamu Munda (Water Serpent)*, Shakira Kelly, 2022, watercolour on paper
Inside cover image: *Burila Munda (Fire Serpent) and Gamu Munda (Water Serpent)*, William Santo 2022; digital art created on iPad
Production management: Christine Bruderlin
Editing: Marg Bowman, Margaret McDonnel
Design and typesetting: Amity Raymont, Elliott Street Typesetting
Photos: as credited
Map: Brenda Thornley

WE GRATEFULLY ACKNOWLEDGE THE SUPPORT OF THE UNIVERSITY OF SYDNEY, BATCHELOR INSTITUTE CENTRE FOR AUSTRALIAN LANGUAGES AND LINGUISTICS AND THE INDIGENOUS LANGUAGES AND ARTS PROGRAM OF THE AUSTRALIAN GOVERNMENT FOR THEIR CONTRIBUTION.

Contents

Preface

My name is William Santo, a traditional owner of the Gudjal nation of Mural (Charters Towers) in Queensland, Australia. Researching and gathering information and material about the Gudjal language has been a long journey. Some old Gudjal speakers were recorded in the early 1970s and these recordings only came to the surface during the Native Title Claim in the early 1990s, when I was gathering evidence of Gudjal people's claim to country. Growing up in my country, I remember older adults talking in a language I didn't know. I wasn't sure if it was Gudjal or another language because some were from the coastal community and others were from Palm Island. I took a keen interest in listening to them talk and trying to understand how they understood each other.

Ricky Santo and the Gudjal boys on Mural (Charters Towers Hill, 1998). (Photo: W Santo)

Over time, my interest in Gudjal language grew. As the King Kiara Community Council coordinator in 1993, I received Peter Sutton's reports and other anthropological reports for our country. I became even more interested in my language and was appointed Chairperson of a new organisation named Inland Land Council in 1995–1996. This organisation looked after all the western inland groups in Hughenden and Richmond. The Inland Land Council became a Prescribed Body Corporate under Mackay's Central Queensland Land Council. I then had the opportunity to work with anthropologists and linguists. I also established a Gudjal traditional owners' corporation around 1999 which enabled Gudjal people to put in a Native Title claim. This opened the door for me to talk to cattle station owners on Gudjal Country to find more written Gudjal language, and I found more in the early diaries from Bluff Downs Station.

Moving forward to 2003, I then had enough Gudjal material to create a Gudjal dictionary. I approached linguist Cassy Nancarrow in Townsville to help. Together we compiled Gudjal recordings and wordlists from all the sources we could find. We also compared the Gudjal language to Gugu-Badhun and Warrongo languages to write the initial *Gudjal dictionary*, which was published in 2006.

When that book came out, I remember our mob was so proud to see their language in the dictionary; and non-Indigenous people living in Charters Towers were a bit surprised to learn we had all these words. People were excited about that dictionary. Local schools and the Dalrymple Shire got on board and wanted me to come up with Gudjal language for the monument near the Dalrymple National Park. It was an exciting time back then, being on my own country after realising that our language was only asleep and needed awakening.

Quite a few people have come up to me and said, 'It's incredible what you've done in reviving your language.' Language is an important part of our identity. As I see it, that dictionary gave our words back to our mob in a new way, in the written form. In this book, the dictionary has been refined and added to by listening again to the old recordings. We have also taken the next step by adding a grammar guide. This book teaches how to put words together to make a sentence. I hope *Yaru! Gudjal learner's guide and dictionary* will be helpful in the community and used by our young people in song and dance. I also hope our people will welcome others to our country in Gudjal and make songs and greetings in Gudjal. Who knows, in the future we might even have fluent speakers!

I am pleased to have met Myfany Turpin. Myfany understood my goal to compile a Gudjal grammar guide for our mob so they could learn their traditional language. That first meeting with Myfany was a highlight for me, and through this, I met Alex Anderson, a master's student at The University of Sydney who worked with me to put this learner's guide together. It's something we Gudjal mob can always use, treasure and be proud of.

I deeply thank the North Queensland Regional Aboriginal Corporation Languages Centre and all the Gudjal people who have supported and encouraged me to keep working on Gudjal language, especially my older cousins Harold, Valerie and the late David, and my daughter Keesha.

William Santo, February 2023

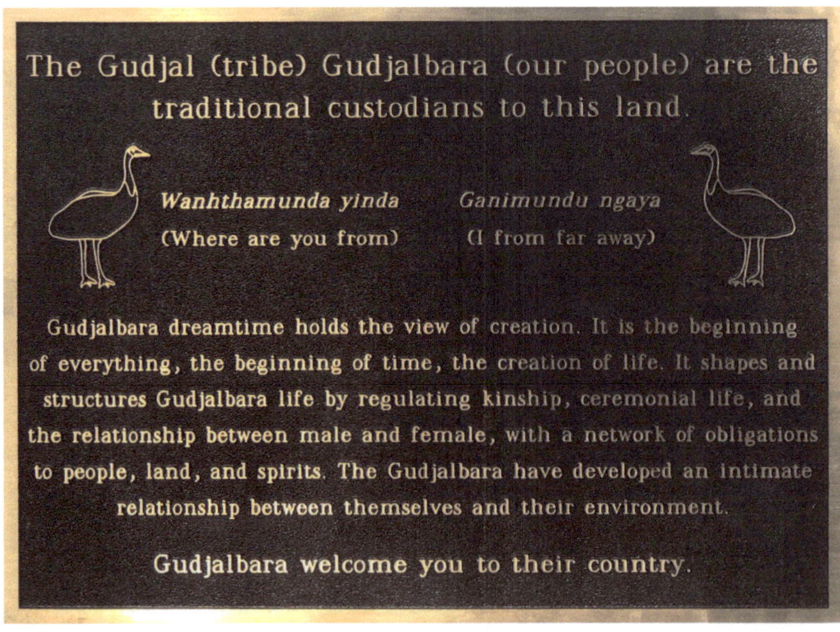

Monument near Dalrymple National Park, Gudjal text by William created around 2000. (Photo: William Santo 2022)

Introduction

This book is a resource for Gudjal people who want to learn their language. It is for Gudjal people who might want to write or sing songs in Gudjal, welcome people in Gudjal and for anyone who wants to learn how to put words together to make sentences and have simple conversations.

The first part of this book focuses on grammar: how to put words together to make sentences and have simple conversations. It includes songs and a Welcome to Country in Gudjal. The sentences, tables, songs and Welcome to Country all have accompanying audio which you can play by scanning the QR codes in this book. You can download the full audio at https://gudjal.bandcamp.com/album/. The audio is archived at the Pacific and Regional Archive for Digital Sources in Endangered Cultures (PARADISEC) at https://catalog.paradisec.org.au/collections/Yaru. To access you must first sign up with PARADISEC as a user at https://catalog.paradisec.org.au/users/sign_up. The second part of this book is a Gudjal dictionary as well as an English to Gudjal finder list and thesaurus. The thesaurus lists Gudjal words by categories such as 'People', 'Parts of the body' and 'Plants'. A list of useful resources is included at the end of the book.

Who wrote this book and why?

This guide is the next step in Gudjal language learning by William Santo. William is the author of many other books about the Gudjal language. These books give an excellent introduction to the rich and varied Gudjal vocabulary. They include *The Gudjal Book of Birds, The Gudjal Book of Animals* and *My Country: in Gudjal and English* (see Further reading and listening on page 115).

The Gudjal language in this book is based on recordings of four Gudjal Elders. They were all stockmen that worked across north Queensland. One was Fred Toomba. His second name is based on a Gudjal word for sheep — **dhumba**. Another was George Reid. He used to be a policeman on Palm Island in the early 1970s. He was William's uncle through the Masso's side. Harry Bunn was a Gudjal and Gugu Badhun speaker and his skin name was Gurrgura. Ranji Pope was a half brother to Harry Bunn. He spent his later life in Charters Towers where his daughter Connie Edwards lived.*

Fred Toomba was recorded on Palm Island and Ranji Pope was recorded in Charters Towers, both in 1970 by Peter Sutton. Harry Bunn was recorded in Townsville in 1974 by Tasaku Tsunoda. George Reid was recorded in Charters Towers in 1970 by Gavan Breen. You can hear more about this time from Peter Sutton and William Santo in the podcast episode 'Buried in the sand: digging deep into Gudjal language and culture' https://anchor.fm/toksave-culture-talks.

* Deceased people are indicated by the cross symbol (†).

William Santo and Gavan Breen in Alice Springs, December 2021. (Photo: M Turpin)

William Santo and Peter Sutton in Adelaide, November 2022. (Photo: W Santo)

Keesha Gordon, Myfany Turpin and Shakira Kelly, Sydney, October 2022. (Photo: A Thorne)

Linguists Peter Sutton, Tasaku Tsunoda and Gavan Breen worked with Gudjal speakers in the 1970s to record the Gudjal language. Peter Sutton and Tasaku Tsunoda also worked very closely with the Gudjal language's closest relatives, Gugu-Badhun and Warrongo. In this book, when we don't know how to say something in Gudjal, we show examples from Sutton's and Tsunoda's work on these languages.

Alex Anderson and William Santo, Sydney, 2022. (Photo: M Turpin)

This book also builds on the work of language teacher Trevor Stockley, who compiled materials for the 2006 Gudjal language workshops run by the North Queensland Regional Aboriginal Corporation Languages Centre (NQRACLC).

Drawing on all this previous work, the learner's guide was put together by Alex Anderson and William Santo in 2021. Alex Anderson did the work as part of his one-year master's in Linguistics at The University of Sydney in 2021. Alex and William did it entirely over Zoom because no one could travel due to COVID-19! You can watch their presentation about this project at https://www.youtube.com/watch?v=4RRbl0A-D6M. You can also hear 50 words in Gudjal read by William at https://50words.online/. Linguists Myfany Turpin and Jakelin Troy at The University of Sydney provided supervision and support for William and Alex's work. They also wrote funding applications to publish this book.

Cassy Nancarrow, Kuranda 2022. (Photo: C Nancarrow)

Linguist Cassy Nancarrow edited and improved on the Gudjal dictionary she and William published in 2003, so that it could be included in this book. Alex added to the dictionary section and Cassy similarly contributed to the learner's guide section. Linguists Dimitrije Karadarevic and Bridey Lea created the English to Gudjal finder list and Myfany helped in writing, editing and managing the project.

Prof Jakelin Troy, from The University of Sydney. (Photo: J Troy)

The sentences are read by Gudjal women Keesha Gordon and Shakira Kelly. Keesha is an educator and musician, and Shakira Kelly is an artist and musician. They travelled to The University of Sydney for one week in October of 2022 to read the Gudjal sentences in this book, with funding from the University of Sydney Indigenous Strategy and Services. They also wrote new songs in Gudjal, working with William, and performed these with Sydney Conservatorium of Music students. They also created much of the artwork that you see in this guide. The spoken audio was edited and mastered by Jacob Craig, at The University of Sydney.

The songs were recorded at Sydney Conservatorium of Music with the Yamalbara Band ('the Rainbow Band'), who are Isabella Chiper, Alysha De Ruyter, Imogen Temple, Keesha Gordon, Shakira Kelly, Myfany Turpin (vocals), Gena Stone (vocals, acoustic guitar), William Santo (vocals, acoustic guitar, clapsticks), Delia O'Kelly (saxophone, keyboard), Roy Valentine (piano), Jackson Williams, Aiden Bowie (electric guitar), Charles Cauduro (drums) and Martin O'Flynn (bass). The didjeridu track, performed by David Hudsen, was recorded in Queensland by Nigel Pegrum. The recordings were mixed by Paul Mac, Jodie Kell, Toby Martin and Imogen Temple.

The Yamalbara Band then performed at Sydney Conservatorium of Music on 27 October 2022. Gudjal Elder Harold Alley, a war veteran, also spoke at this event. The event can be watched on https://youtu.be/U0lG12bkl2k. We thank Anna Thorne for supporting William, Keesha and Shakira in Sydney.

In the next section, we talk about how we wrote this book, and why we did it in the way we did.

Myfany Turpin, Shakira Kelly and Keesha Gordon recording the audio for this book, October 2022. (Photo: W Santo)

Rehearsing in the studio at Sydney Conservatorium of Music, October 2022. (Photo: J Kell)

Yamalbara Band at Sydney Conservatorium of Music, October 2022. (Photo: A Thorne)

William Santo, Keesha Gordon and Shakira Kelly at Sydney Conservatorium of Music, October 2022. (Photo: A Thorne)

Alex, William and Harold at Sydney Conservatorium of Music, October 2022. (Photo: M Turpin)

Language names

A language can have many names and different pronunciations and spellings. For example, Ranji Pope called his language 'Gurdjal' (with an 'r'). Other speakers, like Freddie Toomba, Harry Bunn and George Reid, called their language 'Gudjal'. Another speaker, Alf Palmer, pronounced his language Kuritjal, with three syllables. All of these names are correct. The many names reflect different ways people speak and write. If you know any of these languages by a different name, then keep using that name! We have chosen to use the spelling 'Gudjal' throughout this book because this is the spelling used in other Gudjal language books. We think this will make it easier for people looking for books on Gudjal.

In this book, we also talk about Gugu-Badhun and Warrongo because they are closely related languages to Gudjal. Again, these aren't the only ways of pronouncing or spelling the names. Warrongo is written 'Warungu' or 'Warrungnu' in other places. We use 'Warrongo' because this is what is used in *A Grammar of Warrongo* (Tsunoda 2012).

Gudjal people and country

Gudjal language was traditionally spoken by people who lived in the Charters Towers area, especially along the rivers and around the basalt country where water is plentiful in lagoons all year round. From the 1860s, violent invasion, intensive white settlement and government policy all heavily impacted on Gudjal people. Native Mounted Police who were stationed at Dalrymple and Ravenswood, along with others such as early pastoralists, killed and massacred many Gudjal people. By the 1890s most of the violence of the early frontier had ended and many Gudjal families lived in camps on the edges of stations around Charters Towers where they worked for low or no wages.

In the years following the introduction of the *Aboriginals Protection and Restriction of the Sale of Opium Act* (1897), many Gudjal people were forcibly removed from the Charters Towers area and sent to settlements and missions further afield including Palm Island, Yarrabah, Cherbourg and Woorabinda. However, some families of those who worked on the stations were able to remain on their homelands. Today most Gudjal people live in Charters Towers, Townsville, Cairns and Brisbane, with some living outside of Queensland.

For more history of Gudjal country see *Written true not gammon: a history of Aboriginal Charters Towers* (Babidge et al. 2007) and *Maggie and Charley Santo: the history of the Santo family of Charters Towers* (Santo 2016).

Closely related languages

Why are we including examples from Gugu-Badhun and Warrongo?

In this book, most of the information on Gudjal comes from a handful of original audio recordings of four older men who spoke Gudjal in the 1970s. You can read more about these men on page 1. They are held at the Australian Institute for Aboriginal and Torres Strait Islander Studies (see 'Further Reading & Listening'). Since then, Gudjal hasn't been heard much.

There is a lot of information in these tapes, and we can learn a lot from them. However, for some bits of grammar, there aren't enough examples for us to understand everything.

Map of North Queensland showing where Gudjal and neighbouring languages were traditionally spoken (map does not show language boundaries). (Map: B Thornley)

Sometimes there are differences in the speakers' language, perhaps because of where they had lived or who they spent time with.

Gudjal, Gugu-Badhun and Warrongo are very similar languages, but not the same. Gugu-Badhun and Warrongo are the closest languages to Gudjal though, and for that reason, when we don't have enough information about Gudjal grammar, we have included examples from Gugu-Badhun and Warrongo to help fill in the gaps (we will point out the differences between the languages when they come up). Gugu-Badhun and Warrongo words are in blue font to clearly distinguish these words from Gudjal.

This guide will teach you a lot about Gudjal, but it won't teach you everything. Once you finish reading this guide, you might want to read the technical books about Gugu-Badhun and Warrongo by Sutton (1973) and Tsunoda (2012) listed in Further reading and listening, page 115. These books contain much more information about the languages and will give you a better understanding of how Gudjal might have been spoken.

Was this 'real' Gudjal or was the speaker unsure about how to say it?

At the time of recording, many Gudjal speakers were quite elderly. In some parts of the tapes, you can hear that they clearly had trouble remembering how to say a particular word or sentence in Gudjal. They probably hadn't spoken Gudjal for many, many years! Sometimes they realised when they made a mistake and corrected themselves, but at other times we can't tell how confident they were. Sometimes a person gave two different ways for saying the same thing. For example, on one occasion a Gudjal speaker translated 'my brother' as **ngaya mugina** (literally 'I brother') and then a bit later he translated it as **ngaygu mugina** (literally 'my brother').

Because we have so few examples, we don't always know what to make of these differences. Could they both be correct ways of saying 'my brother'? Is only one of these ways correct? If so, which one?

In this guide, we have done our best to try and find the most representative ways of speaking, and to present these in an easy-to-understand way. However, sometimes we just don't know how something was said. With more people using and talking about Gudjal, we think new, standard ways of speaking will fall into place.

Even within the same language, different speakers have different ways of saying things

Different people have different ways of speaking — even when they're using the same language. You might notice this in English. Maybe your friend or family member has a word or expression they always use. It might be because they're from a particular part of the country, or a particular age, or it might be some other reason. This also happens in Gudjal. Some speakers prefer to use particular grammar, and particular words. Because of this, we have included the name of the speaker who the example comes from. If you know that you have a closer connection to one of the speakers in this guide, then you might like to learn their way of speaking.

Different ways of speaking

Harry Gertz, a Gugu-Badhun Elder and speaker of Gugu-Badhun, once said that Gudjal speakers have a 'Yankee drawl'. Peter Sutton says that he might be talking about the way that some Gudjal speakers made words longer by adding a **ra** or a **la** at the end of them. Freddie Toomba (FT) did this, but Ranji Pope (RP) and Harry Bunn (HB) didn't tend to do this. Have a look at these examples:

Table 1. Different ways of saying words (adding -la or -ra)

Gudjal (FT)	Gudjal (RP* and HB*)	English
gaya**la**	**gaya**	'father'
buri**la**	**buri**	'fire'
yara**la**	**yara**	'man'
gari**la**	**gari**	'sun'
yamba**la**	**yamba**	'camp'
warngu**ra**	**warngu**	'woman'
bangga**la**	**banggay**	'spear'

*These words are also in Gugu-Badhun, with the exception of **buri** and **yara**.

At the moment, we think these are just different ways of saying the same word. We don't think the **la** or **ra** endings change anything in the grammar.

Freddie Toomba's Gudjal is also different to other varieties of Gudjal in other ways. For example, he uses different word endings for the past (**-na**) and the present (**-ya**). Other Gudjal speakers used the same word ending for both (**-n**), but we will explain this further in section 5.4, page 42.

If you know how to say something in Gudjal, keep doing it your way!

You might already know how to say some things in Gudjal. Maybe you heard family or community members saying it a certain way. Sometimes your way of saying something will be different to what this guide says. This doesn't mean that your way is wrong. The aim of this book is to describe how Ranji Pope, Freddie Toomba, George Reid and Harry Bunn spoke Gudjal in the 1970s. But languages are always changing, and what's important is to build on what you know. So keep saying it your way with pride and take from this guide what is helpful to you.

Learner's Guide

Bundjibara
'plum tree'

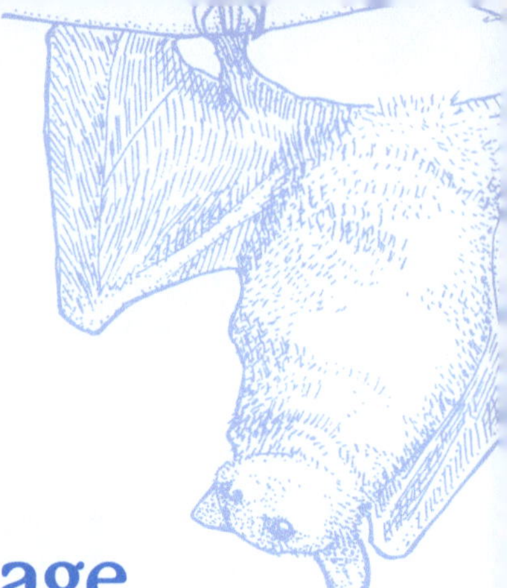

1 Learning Gudjal Language

This part of the book will teach you how to put words together to make sentences — grammar. It consists of nine chapters. In these you will learn some tips for language learning, the sounds of Gudjal, greetings, nouns, verbs and other aspects of grammar such as asking questions. You will also learn about word endings and pronouns and Gudjal skin names. The final chapter of this learner's guide gives four Gudjal songs and a Welcome to Country.

In this chapter, we give you some tips which will help you learn a language, show you how Gudjal sentences are presented, and introduce some grammar terms that will help you learn how to put Gudjal words together.

1.1 Language learning tips

This section gives you some general tips to help you learn a language and remember words.

Make stories about words

When you learn a new word in Gudjal, make a little story out of it. Normally, if you try just to memorise a word, your brain has a hard time remembering the connection. In the example that follows, the words 'sun' and **gari** sound nothing alike. But by making up a short story that connects these two words, your brain has an easier time making a connection between them. It doesn't matter what these stories are. As long as they make sense to you, they will help you learn and remember new words.

Using a story works extra well if you link the story to your life. For example, the word for 'sun' in Gudjal is **gari.** The word **gari** sounds a bit like the word 'curry' in English. I love curry, so sometimes when I look up at the sun, I like to imagine it turning into a big bowl of nice spicy red curry. Now I have a connection between the meaning of the word **gari** and the sound of the word (a bit like 'curry'). Another example is the word for 'belly', which in Gudjal is **bamba**. The word **bamba** sounds a bit like 'bumbag'. Where do I wear a bumbag? Generally, around my belly.

Repeat, repeat, repeat

It's easy to forget a new word, but if we relearn a word just before we're about to forget it, then we remember it even better (and for even longer). So, to do this, we need to repeat words regularly. Try practising words every morning and night, even if it's just for five minutes. If you only study every Wednesday, for example, even if you spend several hours studying, you will have forgotten everything you learnt the previous Wednesday! Repetition and frequency are the keys when learning a language.

1.2 Gudjal example sentences

Throughout this part of the book, you are going to see and hear a lot of Gudjal example sentences, so it's useful to know how we present them. Have a look at the diagram below.

Audio

The number and QR code shows that there is accompanying audio which you can hear by scanning the QR code. The audio is read by Keesha, Shakira or William; and the songs are performed by the Yamalbara Band. You can also download and listen to the entire audio (144 tracks) at https://gudjal.bandcamp.com/album/yaru-gudjal-learner-s-guide-and-dictionary. You can then listen to the audio offline or practice without the book.

Gudjal sentence

The top line of examples is a Gudjal sentence. Some Gudjal sentences include **bold** words to highlight the word or ending that is shown by the example. (The example below is from section 4.1 where we explain that there are no words for 'a' and 'the', you just say the word on its own — that's why **gaygara** 'kangaroo' is in bold). Hyphens are used in the examples to distinguish a word from an ending; however, when writing Gudjal hyphens aren't usually used.

English equivalent

This is placed underneath each Gudjal word. Endings, such as **-na**, are translated with capital letters; -PAST isn't a literal translation. The capital letters just tell you what the word ending is doing. In this example, it's putting the action in the past, so we use -PAST to translate the word ending. A list of all the word ending translations used in this book is given in Table 2 (next page).

Translation

The line in quote marks is an English free translation of the sentence. Sometimes we give more than one free translation. These are separated by the symbol '/'.

Recording and speaker

The bottom row gives the name of the original audio file and speaker. For example, this sentence is on the audio file 'SUTTON_P01-001913B'. The audio was originally recorded by Peter Sutton with Gudjal speaker Freddie Toomba (FT). A few examples are from fieldnotes that have no matching audio on the recording, perhaps because the tape had run out, or the battery had gone flat. These are marked '(extra transcript)'.

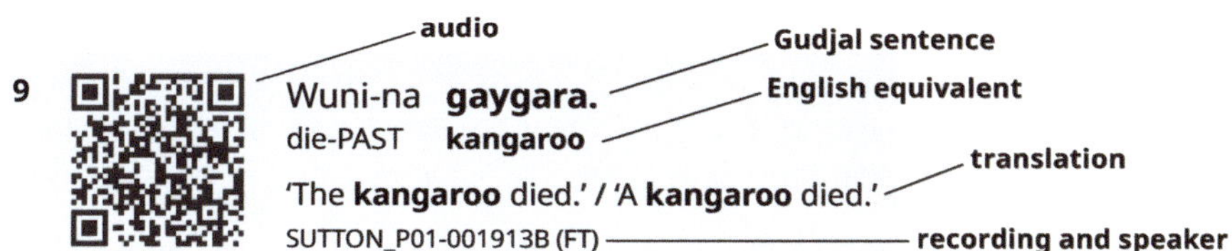

Table 2. List of abbreviations used to translate word endings

Abbreviation	Linguistic term	Meaning	Gudjal
-CONT	continuous	the action continues	**-li**
-DOER	ergative; agent	doer; actor (see section 4.7, page 31)	**-nggu**
-EMPH	emphatic	adds emphasis to what you are saying	**-giya**
-FROM	ablative	'from'	**-mundu/-ngumay(a)**
-LOC	locative	'at', 'in', 'on'	**-ngga/-da/-nda/ -ndja/-ba**
-MIGHT	subjunctive	'might', 'could', 'would', 'will'	**-yngga**
-ORDER	imperative	gives an order or command	**-ya**
-PAST	past tense	the action happened in the past	**-na**
-PAST/PRES	non-future tense	the action is happening now OR in the past	**-n/-y/-l**
-POSS	possessive; genitive	'belongs to'	**-na**
-PRES	present tense	the action is happening now	**-ya**
-REASON	participle of purpose	'in order to do something'	**-nyu**
-REP	iterative	the action happens repeatedly	**-nda**
-TO/FOR	dative	'to', 'for'	**-wu/-gu**
-WILL	future tense	the action will happen	**-gu**
-WITH	instrumental	'using', 'with'	**-nggu**

Each row in this table has its own dedicated section, so don't worry about understanding everything now.

Things still to work out

This doesn't have to do with grammar, but when you see ### below a word, as in Example 1, it means we don't know the meaning of this word or ending. We still need to do more research.

1 

Guyba-ya-nyu bimu-wu.
give-ORDER-### aunty-TO/FOR
'Give (it) to aunty.'
SUTTON_P01-001913B (FT)

Additionally, in this guide we have tried to use as many example sentences from the original recordings as possible. However, sometimes we just don't know how something would have been said. In these cases, we have included an example which doesn't come from the recordings. This example is made by us, and is based on our understanding of how Gudjal works. In these cases, instead of providing the name of the original recording or page number, we have written (New example').

For example:

2 

Mural-mundu ngaya.
Mural-from I

'I'm from Mural (Charters Towers).'
(New example)

1.3 Some useful grammar terms

To learn about Gudjal grammar, we have to know some words that talk about grammar. In this section, we explain what nouns, verbs, pronouns and word endings are.

Nouns

A noun is usually a person, place or thing. When we think of nouns, we usually think of things that we can touch or see or hear. Here are some examples of nouns: 'woman', 'man', 'cat', 'house', 'chair', 'fire', 'country', 'bird', 'spear'.

Another way to find nouns is to look at the words around them. In English, a noun usually has a word like 'the', 'a' or 'some' before it. The following underlined words are nouns:

The tree
A table
Some food

Pronouns

Pronouns are words like 'I', 'me', 'you', 'he', 'him', 'she', 'her', 'us', 'it', etc. They can replace nouns.

If I wanted to tell a story about James, I might say this: 'James went to the shops. He bought a shirt. Then he went home.' The word 'he' stands for 'James'.

If we said: 'James went to the shops. James bought a shirt. Then James went home.', it would sound a bit repetitive and strange. That's why we use pronouns.

Adjectives

Adjectives are describing words. They tell us about a noun. The following underlined words are adjectives:

A black dog.
Her big belly.
The good boy.
That spear is sharp.
They are cheeky.

In Gudjal, nouns, pronouns and adjectives all work in similar ways. We will learn more about this in section 4.8.

Verbs

A verb is a doing word. It describes an action or event. The following underlined words are verbs:

> I <u>went</u> to the shops.
> You <u>ate</u> my food.
> She <u>climbed</u> the hill.
> The dog <u>bit</u> the man.
> We <u>carried</u> the box.

Another way to identify English verbs is that they'll sometimes have a special verb ending, like '-ed' or '-ing'. For example:

> I watch<u>ed</u> some TV.
> I am go<u>ing</u> to bed.

Word endings

Word endings are little bits of language that have certain meanings. For example, in English the '-s' word ending can mean that there are lots of something. When we say 'cat', we think of one cat, but when we say 'cat<u>s</u>' with the '-s' ending, we think of more than one cat.

These endings can't exist on their own, and they must attach to the ends of other words. Gudjal has lots of these word endings, which can also be called suffixes.

Rickie Santo and Gudjal dancers at Mural (Charters Towers), 1998. (Photo: William Santo)

2 The sounds of Gudjal

Gudjal has its own sounds and alphabet. Most of the letters used to write Gudjal make the same sounds as in English. Some are different, though. Some of these explanations come from the *Gudjal dictionary*. There are two kinds of sounds: vowels and consonants.

2.1 Consonants

Letter	Word	Sound
b	**b**alanu 'moon'	Like the 'b' in 'baby', although at the start of words it can sound like 'p'.
d	ga**d**a 'head'	Like the 'd' in 'dog', although at the start of words it can sound like 't'.
dh	**dh**anha 'they'	Like the letter 'd', but with our tongue touching our teeth. At the start of the word, it can sound a bit like 't'.
dj	ba**dj**i 'full'	A bit like the 'j' in 'jump' or the 'ch' in 'chomp', but with more of our tongue touching the roof of our mouth.
g	wa**g**al 'eel'	Like the 'g' in 'go', although at the start of words it can sound like 'k'.
k	gun**k**a 'raw'	This is pronounced like the 'g' above. We use this letter to avoid mix-ups (see the notes on page 18).
l	ngi**l**an 'girl'	Like the 'l' in 'lolly'.
m	**m**ari 'Aboriginal person'	Like the 'm' in 'mouse'.
n	mugi**n**a 'brother'	Like the 'n' in 'nose'.
ng	**ng**ani 'who'	Like the 'ng' in 'singing'.
nh	**nh**ani 'ground'	Like the 'n' sound, but with our tongue touching our teeth.
ny	gi**ny**u 'baby'	Like the 'ny' in 'canyon'.
r	ya**r**a 'man'	Like the 'r' in 'rose'.
rr	ya**rr**aman 'horse'	A tapped or trilled 'r' like in Italian or Scottish English.
w	**w**agal 'eel'	Like the 'w' in 'water'.
y	**y**uri 'meat'	Like the 'y' in 'yes'.

The letter 'y' can be used in combination with vowels to create new sounds.

ay	g**ay**bal 'fire'	Like the 'ay' in 'day' or the 'igh' in 'sigh'
uy	yag**uy** 'skin'	Like the 'oy' in 'boy'

The letter 'k' is used to distinguish between a few different consonant combinations.

ng	ya**ng**a 'mother'	Like the 'ng' sound in 'singing'.
ngg	ba**ngg**ala 'spear'	Like the 'ng' sound in 'finger'.
nk	ga**nk**ari 'knife'	Like the 'n' and 'g' sound in 'sun-garden'.

Note: Don't confuse **ng** (one sound) with **ngg** (two sounds) or **nk** (two sounds):

> 'ng' as in **yanga** 'mother': 'ng' is one sound, the same as 'ng' in English 'singing';
> 'ngg' as in **banggala** 'spear': 'ngg' is two sounds: 'ng' and 'g' together, as in English 'finger'.
> 'nk' as in **gankari** 'knife': 'nk' is two sounds: 'n' and 'g' together, as in English 'sun-garden';

The sounds 'nh' and 'dh' often go together; but writing 'nhdh' looks a bit long and confusing, so we have simplified it to 'ndh'.

So, if you ever see the letter 'n' come right before 'dh', remember that it is pronounced as 'nh'. In the following example, the 'n' in **wandha** is pronounced as 'nh' (with our tongue touching our teeth).

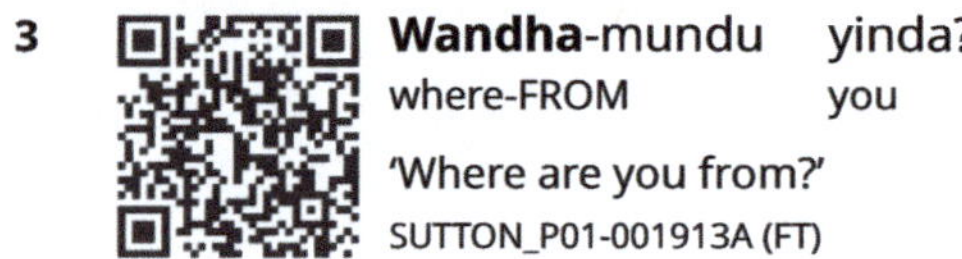

3 **Wandha**-mundu yinda?
where-FROM you
'Where are you from?'
SUTTON_P01-001913A (FT)

2.2 Vowels

Letter	Word	Sound
a	b**a**l**a**nu 'moon'	like the 'a' in 'father' or the 'ar' in 'cart'
i	mar**i** 'Aboriginal person'	like the 'i' in 'bit' or 'winter'
u	w**u**may 'good'	like the 'u' in 'put' or the 'oo' in 'good'

2.3 Stress

A syllable is a 'chunk' of a word. Most Gudjal words have at least two syllables:

> **yaru** ('hello', 'here', 'this') has two syllables: **ya-ru**.
> **banggala** ('spear') has three syllables: **bang-ga-la**.
> **gayimbula** ('cockatoo') has four syllables: **ga-yim-bu-la**.

We usually put stress (emphasis) on the first syllable in Gudjal words:

YA-ru	not **ya-RU**
BANG-ga-la	not **bang-GA-la**
GA-yim-bu-la	not **ga-YIM-bu-la** or **ga-yim-BU-la**

Special rules

If you learn how to pronounce the letters in the way we set out in at the beginning of this section (2.3), that is fantastic. These rules will give you great pronunciation.

But there are also some special rules which will help make your Gudjal sound even more like the old people in the tapes. Only learn the following rules after you've mastered the rules that we laid out at the beginning of this section (2.3).

No 'w'

- When a word starts with the letters 'wu', like in **wulan** ('he died', HB), speakers sometimes left off the 'w'. So, it would have sounded like 'ulan'.
- Speakers left the 'w' on when it came before a vowel that wasn't 'u'. So **walwa** ('bad', RP) always just sounded like **walwa**.

3 Greeting people in Gudjal

In English, we often spend some time at the start of a conversation talking about nothing. When you think about it, phrases like 'hello' and 'how are you?' don't actually have a lot of meaning. For example, when we ask someone — especially a stranger — how they are, we expect that they'll answer with 'Good, thanks. And you?' If a stranger answered with 'I'm terrible!' and then told you why they were feeling terrible, we would think that they were a bit strange.

This greeting happens in a lot of European languages, but it doesn't happen in every language. For this reason, we don't have an *exact* translation of the words for 'hello' and 'how are you?'.

Here are some basic greetings and introductions you could use in Gudjal.

Yaru!
(Hello!)

Yandjaya ngubiya yinda!
(Come and tell me.)

Banggala mugaya,
yuriwu ngali yaniya.
(Bring a spear, let's us
two go for meat.)

4 

Yaru!
here
'(I'm) here.' / 'Hello!'
SUTTON_P01-001913B (FT)

5 

Wandha-mundu yinda?
where-FROM you
'Where are you from?'
SUTTON_P01-001913A (FT)

6 

Mural-mundu ngaya.
Mural-FROM I
'I'm from Charters Towers.'
(New example)

7 

Ngani yinda?
who you
'What is your name?' / 'Who are you?'
(New example)

8 

Ngaya Keesha/Shakira.
I Keesha/Shakira
'My name is Keesha/Shakira.' / 'I am Keesha/Shakira.'
(New example)

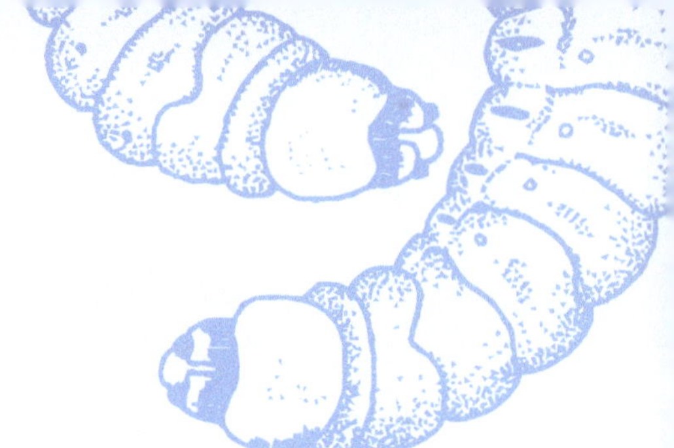

4 Nouns, pronouns, adjectives

In this chapter we focus on nouns and noun endings and don't really look at verb endings. For now, don't worry too much about understanding the endings that follow verbs (e.g. 'die', 'get', 'give', etc.). These will make more sense as you read on.

4.1 'The' and 'a'

There are no words like 'the', 'a' or 'an' in Gudjal. If you want to say 'the kangaroo' or 'a kangaroo', you just say 'kangaroo'.

9 

Wuni-na **gaygara.**
die-PAST **kangaroo**

'**The kangaroo** died.'/'**A kangaroo** died.'
SUTTON_P01-001913B (FT)

4.2 Using things: 'with a . . .'

To say that you did something *using something*, such as 'hit it *with a stick*', we use an ending. We add **-nggu** to the end of the thing that was used.

10 

Banggala-nggu muga-na ngaya.
spear-WITH get-PAST I

'I got it **with the spear**.'/'I got it **using a spear**.'
SUTTON_P01-001913B (FT)

11 

Mara-nggu muga-ya manu-ngga.
hand-WITH get-ORDER neck/throat-LOC

'Get (the bone out) **with your hand** down your throat!'/
'Get (the bone out) **using your hand** down your throat!'
SUTTON_P01-001912A (RP)

4.3 'To' and 'for'

In Gudjal, there are no separate words for 'to' and 'for'. Instead, we use the ending -**wu** on the noun.

To say that you are giving something 'to' someone, **-wu** goes on the word for the person you are giving it to.

12	Guyba-ya-nyu	**bimu-wu.**
	give-ORDER-###	**aunty-TO/FOR**

'Give (it) **to aunty**.'
SUTTON_P01-001913B (FT)

To say that you are going 'to' a place, **-wu** goes on the word for the place you are going to.

13	Yani-gu	**yamba-wu.**
	come/go-WILL	**camp-TO/FOR**

'(I am) going **home**'/'**to the camp**.'
TSUNODA_T08-003412B (HB)

14	**Yambala-wu**	gandji-ya	ngali.
	camp/home-TO/FOR	take/carry-ORDER	we two

'Let's take it **to camp**!'/'How about me and you take it **to camp**?'
SUTTON_P01-001913A (FT)

15	**Yamba-wu**	yani-na	ngaya.
	camp/home-TO/FOR	go-PAST	I

'I went back **to camp.**'
SUTTON_P01-001913B (FT)

To say that you are going 'for' something or some reason, such as to get something, **-wu** goes on the thing you are getting.

16	**Gaygara-wu**	yani-yngga	ngaya.
	kangaroo-TO/FOR	come/go-MIGHT	I

'I'm going out **for a kangaroo**.'
SUTTON_P01-001913B (FT)

Fast speech

Often, speakers didn't pronounce the 'w' in **-wu** when they were speaking quickly. So **bimuwu** 'for aunty' or 'to aunty' would have sounded like **bimuu** or **bimu**. **Gaygarawu** 'for kangaroo' would have sounded like **gaygarau**. When speakers were asked to repeat themselves, or when they spoke slowly, they often pronounced the 'w'. That's how we know it is there.

Careful!

This ending actually has two forms, but they both mean the same thing. It's like the words 'a' and 'an' in 'a dog' and 'an apple' in English. They mean the same thing, but 'a' comes before consonants, and 'an' comes before vowels.

The form **-wu** comes after a word that ends in a vowel (a, i, u), as we have just seen.

The form **-gu** is used after a word that ends in a consonant (all other letters). We don't have any examples of this in Gudjal, but here is one from Gugu-Badhun.

17 

Dhulay **gaybal-gu.**
wood **fire-TO/FOR**

'The wood is **for the fire.**'
Sutton 1973, p 120

Even though this was said by a Gugu-Badhun speaker, the words **dhulay** 'wood, tree, stick' and **gaybal** 'fire' are also Gudjal words.

If you want to say it's 'for' someone, or it's going 'to' someone (e.g. 'to me', 'to you', 'to her'), then you can use a 'to/for' pronoun. We don't have evidence of these pronouns in Gudjal (except for 'to/for me'), so we have shown the Warrongo pronouns. In the following, the pronouns in black are Gudjal, and the rest are from Warrongo.

'To' and 'for' pronouns

18

Hear all 'to' and 'for' pronouns.

Talking about ourselves:

'to/for me'	ngaygu**nda**
'to/for us two'	ngali**ngunku**
'to/for all of us'	ngana**ngunku**

Talking about the person we're speaking to:

'to/for you (one person)'	yin**dana**
'to/for you two'	yubala**ngunku**, yinu**ngunku**
'to/for you lot'	yurra**ngunku**

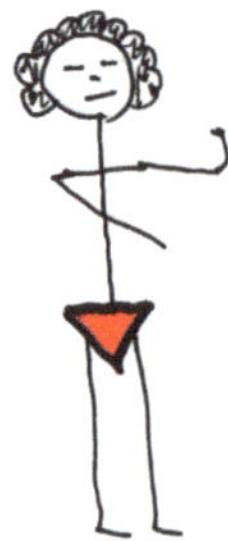

Talking about other people:

'to/for him/her/its'	nyu**ngunku**
'to/for them (two)'	bula**ngunku**
'to/for them (all of them)'	djana**ngunku**

Here's an example of a 'to/for' pronoun in use.

19

Nhula yani **ngaygunda.**
he come **to me**

'He might come **here.**'/'He's coming **to me.**'
SUTTON_P01-001912A (RP)

4.4 'From' somewhere

To say 'from' a place, you use an ending after the word for the place. There are three different endings you can use: **-mundu**, **-ngumay** and **-ngumaya.**

We don't have any examples of one speaker using both **-mundu** and **-ngumay(a)** in their language. Freddie Toomba used **-mundu** while other speakers recorded used **-ngumay(a)**.

20

Wandha-mundu	yinda?
where-FROM	you

'Where are you **from**?'/**'Where** do you come **from**?'
SUTTON_P01-001913A (FT)

21

Gani-mundu.	Ngayngarra.
far-FROM	cheeky

'(They're) **from far away**. (They're) cheeky.'/
'(They came) **from far away**. (They're) cheeky.'
SUTTON_P01-001913B (FT)

22

Wandja-ngumay	yinda?
where-FROM	you

'Where are you **from**?'/**'Where** do you come **from**?'
Tsunoda 1974, MS709 (HB)

23

Yamba-ngumaya.
camp-FROM

'(He's coming) **from home/camp.**'
SUTTON_P01-001911B (RP)

24

Milili	nhaga-na	ngaya	**ngarra,**	**burila-mundu.**
light	see-PAST	I	up there	**fire-FROM**

'I saw a light up there, **coming from a fire.**'/
'I saw light up there, **coming out of a fire.**'
SUTTON_P01-001913A (FT)

There are also a set of pronouns for this word ending. Use these when you want to say, 'from me' or 'from them', etc. All of these pronouns come from Warrongo.

'From' pronouns

Talking about ourselves:

from me	ngaygu**ngumay**
from us two	ngali**ngumay**
from all of us	ngana**ngumay**

25

Hear all 'from' pronouns.

Talking about the person we're speaking to:

'from you' (one person)	yinu**ngumay**
'from you two'	yubala**ngumay**
'from you lot' (more than two)	yurra**ngumay**

Talking about other people:

'from him/her/it'	nyungu**ngumay**
'from them two'	bula**ngumay**
'from them lot' (more than two)	djana**ngumay**

4.5 Where something happened: 'in', 'on' and 'at'

When we're telling stories, it's very important to know the location where events took place. Did they happen at school? On the bus? In the bush? Gudjal doesn't use different words for 'in', 'on' or 'at', instead it uses a 'location' ending on the word for where something happens. This covers all three meanings: 'in', 'on' and 'at', and can also mean 'in the general area of' or 'next to'. The location ending has five different forms: **-ngga**, **-da**, **-nda**, **-ba** and **-dja**, depending on the word it joins to.

When it joins onto a word that ends in a vowel, the location ending to use is **-ngga**, like **yaru-ngga** 'in/on here'.

26

Yaru-ngga	nyina-ya!
here-LOC	sit-ORDER

'Sit down **here**!'/'Sit down **on here**!'

SUTTON_P01-001913B (FT)

27

Banggala	gadju-na	**gaygara-ngga.**
spear	be stuck-PAST	**kangaroo-LOC**

'The spear was stuck **in the kangaroo**.'

SUTTON_P01-001913B (FT)

When it joins onto a word that ends in the 'l' sound (like in **djambal** 'snake'), the location ending to use is **-da**.

[NO AUDIO AVAILABLE]

Warngu	birri	**djambal-da**	djana-n.
woman	near	**snake-LOC**	stand-PAST/PRES

The woman is standing **alongside a snake**./
The woman stood **next to a snake**.

TSUNODA_T06-002935A (HB)

We don't have examples of this ending on every Gudjal word. Gugu-Badhun and Warrongo help us fill in the gaps and give us an idea of how Gudjal language probably worked.

In Gugu-Badhun, when the word ends in the 'n' sound (like in **mungan** 'mountain'), the location ending is also **-da.**

28 

Nhula ngara yani-n **mungan-da.**
he high go-PAST/PRES **mountain-LOC**

'He went up **the mountain**.'/'He went up high **on the mountain**.'
(Gugu-Badhun) Sutton 1973, p 119

In Gugu-Badhun, when the word ends in the 'y' sound (like in **dhulay** 'tree') the location ending is **-nda.**

29 

dhulay-nda
tree-LOC

'**in** the tree'/'**at** the tree'
(Gugu-Badhun) Sutton 1973, p 117

In Warrongo, when the word ends in the 'm' sound the location ending is **-ba**.

30 

djudjam-ba
locust-LOC

'**on** the locust'/'**next to** the locust'
(Warrongo) Tsunoda 2011, p 166

In Warrongo, when the word ends in the 'ny' sound the location ending is **-dja**.

31 

giyany-dja
mussel shell-LOC

'**on** the mussel shell'
(Warrongo) Tsunoda 2011, p 166

Word ends in...	Word ending	Example
a, i, u	**-ngga**	**gaygara-ngga** 'in the kangaroo'
l, n	**-da**	**djambal-da** 'next to the snake'
y	**-nda**	**dhulay-nda** 'at the tree'
m	**-ba**	**djudjam-ba** 'on the locust'
ny	**-dja**	**giyany-dja** 'on the mussel shell'

Simplifying things

Many, but not all, speakers of Gudjal, Gugu-Badhun and Warrongo said things this way. One speaker of Gugu-Badhun, Richard Hoolihan, used the **-ngga** word ending for every word.

Linguist Peter Sutton believes that using **-ngga** for every word was a newer way of speaking. Using the different word endings (**-ngga, -da,** etc.) was a more traditional way of speaking.

Both ways are correct, because they both come from people who grew up using the language. Whether you choose to use the traditional way (**-ngga, -da,** etc.) or the newer way (**-ngga** for everything) is up to you. We explained the traditional way first, because more people used this way in the recordings.

More information

You may notice in some later examples that speakers sometimes used **-wu** 'to' instead of **-ngga** 'at' to say 'at home', for example. Speakers of Gudjal, Gugu-Badhun and Warrongo could use different noun endings to express similar things (especially when talking about positions). However, for the purposes of learning Gudjal, it might be easier just to remember **-ngga** means 'at' and **-wu** means 'to' or 'for'.

4.6 Possession: whose is it?

'Whose is it?' It is Mary's! In English, this 's' word ending with an apostrophe (') tells us who an item belongs to. In Gudjal, we also use a word ending; however, we still need to do more research on this part of the grammar.

From what we've seen, it is likely that Gudjal has a similar — or the same — word ending as in Gugu-Badhun and Warrongo. In these languages, it is **-ngu**.

32

gaygara-ngu dhumbi
kangaroo-POSS tail
'the kangaroo's tail'/'the tail **of the kangaroo'**
(New example)

33 

warngura-ngu djinggurang
woman-POSS pubic hair
'the woman's hair'/'the hair **of the woman'**
(New example)

> ***Careful!***
> Don't get this **-ngu** (POSS) ending mixed up with the **-nggu** ('with/using') ending. They are different endings, and they are pronounced differently.

'To have'

Gudjal, Gugu-Badhun and Warrongo didn't have a specific word for 'have' (as in 'I have a brother'). They generally used a possessive pronoun or the 'possession' ending **-ngu** to say things like this.

34 

Yinu banggala.
your spear
'This spear **is yours.'** / **'You have** a spear.'
(New example) based on Gugu-Badhun, Sutton 1973, p 127

In Warrongo, speakers could sometimes use the word **'gandji'** 'carry/take' to mean 'have', but usually only when they're talking about a body part. We don't know a lot about this word. To say 'I have' (body part), you might also choose to use **gandji**.

35 

Warngura-nggu	**gandji-ya**	mindjan	dharibara.
woman-DOER	**carry-PRES**	skin	good

'The woman **has** nice skin.'
(New example) based on Warrongo, Tsunoda 2011, p 665

Possessive pronouns

To say 'my', 'her', 'their', etc., we use a possessive pronoun. This describes the person to whom something or someone belongs.

36 

ngaygu	mugina
my	brothers

'**my** brothers'
SUTTON_P01-001912A (RP)

In the following, the pronouns in black are from Gudjal, and the rest are from Warrongo.

Talking about ourselves:

'my'	**ngaygu**
'our' (two)	**ngalingu**
'our' (more than two)	**nganhangu**

37 Hear all the possessive pronouns.

Talking about the person we're speaking to:

'your' (one person)	**yinu**
'your' (two)	**yubalangu**
'your' (more than two)	**yurrangu**

Talking about other people:

'his/her/its'	**nyungu**
'their' (two)	**bulangu**
'their' (more than two)	**dhanangu**

Possessive pronouns can also be used for 'to' and 'for'

In section 4.3, we talked about using the 'to' and 'for' pronouns to say something is going *to someone*. But in Gudjal, you can also use the possessive pronouns for this.

38 

Wayngu-giya.	Ngalnga	guyba-ya	**dhanangu.**
bad-EMPH	don't	give-ORDER	**to them**

'Hey! They're bad. Don't give **them** (anything)!'/
'They're bad! Don't give anything **to them**!'
SUTTON_P01-001913B (FT)

Talking about body parts

In a lot of Australian languages, it's common to talk about body parts without having to mention who they belong to. Usually, context tells us what body part a person is talking about.

39 

Mara-nggu	muga-ya	manu-ngga.
hand-WITH	get-ORDER	throat-LOC

'Get (the bone out) of (your) throat **with (your) hand**!'/
'Get (the bone out) of (your) throat **using (your) hand**!'
SUTTON_P01-001912A (RP)

40 

Mara	muga	yinda.
hand	grab	you

'Grab **(his) hand**!'
(Warrongo) Tsunoda 2011, p 381

However, when we *do* mention *who* the body part belongs to, the 'doer pronoun' is often used (we talk about 'doer pronouns' in section 4.7).

41 

Ngaya	**gadja**	bari-li-n.
I	**head**	twist

'**My head** is twisted.' / '**I** have a **head**ache.'
(Warrongo) Tsunoda 2011, p 532

However, the possessive pronoun is also used sometimes too, like it is in English.

42 

Nguni	**djumbi**	**nyungu.**
there	**tail**	**his**

'There is **his tail**!'
(Warrongo) Tsunoda 2011, p 641

We don't have any examples of this in Gudjal, so we can't tell you what you *should* or *shouldn't* say. However, using either the doer or the possessive pronoun (or even no pronoun at all!) would be a good place to start.

4.7 Who does what in a sentence?

In English we know who is doing an action and who the action is done to by the order of the words. For example, in the sentence 'The dog bit the man', 'the dog' is the *doer* (the subject) of the action and 'the man' is the *receiver*, the person or thing that an action is done to. We know this because the words 'the dog' come before the word 'bit'.

In English, we show who the *doer* of the action is by the order of the words. In an active sentence the doer goes before the verb, for example (using the verb 'bite'):

> 'The man bit the dog.'

Although this sentence isn't as common, we know it's the man who used his teeth to bite the dog, because 'the man' comes before 'bit'. In a passive sentence ('was bitten') the order is switched: the doer goes after the verb and is preceded by the preposition 'by':

> 'The dog was bitten by the man'.

In a passive sentence the doer is often left out altogether: 'the dog was bitten'.

In Gudjal, we don't use the order of words to express who the doer is and who the receiver is. Instead, we use a special word ending **-nggu** on the doer. We don't have to add any special word ending to the receiver. We can use the word as it appears in the dictionary. In 'The dog bit the man' example that follows, the word for 'dog' has the **-nggu** ending and the word for 'man' doesn't have any ending.

43

Gandura-nggu	badha-nda-li	yarala.
dog-DOER	bit-REP-CONT	man

'**The dog bit** the man.'/'It was **the dog that bit** the man.'/
'**The dog is biting** the man.'

SUTTON_P01-001913A (extra transcript) (FT)

44 

Mugina-nggu	miranga-na	banggala	birrgalbay.
brother-DOER	make-PAST	spear	sharp

'**My brother** made a sharp spear.'/'The **brother** made the sharp spear.'/
'**Brother** made a sharp spear.'

SUTTON_P01-001913B (FT)

You might have noticed that our **-nggu** ending here is the same as the **-nggu** ending used to mean 'with' or 'using'. So what do we do if we want to have both endings in the same sentence?

We don't have a lot of examples of sentences with **-nggu** in Gudjal. However, there are some examples from Warrongo, and in cases like these, we just use both endings normally. Context should tell us which one is the doer, and which one is the thing they do it with.

45 

Warrngu-nggu	nyunya	djingga-lgu	**barri-nggu.**
woman-DOER	him	will punch	**stone-WITH**

'**The woman** will punch him **with a stone**.'/
'**The woman** is going to hit him **with a stone**.'

(Warrongo) Tsunoda 2011, p 188

Changing the words around

Although the word order here is the same as in English, in Gudjal either the doer or the receiver can come first. In many languages with 'loose' word order, you put whichever word you want to emphasise first.

So, for example, we could say the following sentences and they would all mean 'brother made a sharp spear'. The only difference between the sentences is what the speaker wants to highlight or emphasise. The emphasised word comes at the beginning.

46

Miranga-na	mugina-nggu	banggala	birrgalbay.
make-PAST	brother-DOER	spear	sharp

'Brother **made** the sharp spear.'
(New example) based on SUTTON_P01-001913B (FT)

Putting **miranga-na** at the start of the sentence emphasises that 'Brother made the sharp spear (he didn't break it, as you might have thought).'

47 

Mugina-nggu	banggala	birrgalbay	mirangana.
brother-DOER	spear	sharp	make-PAST

'**Brother** made the sharp spear.'
(New example) based on SUTTON_P01-001913B (FT)

Putting **mugina-nggu** at the start of the sentence emphasises that 'It was brother (and not sister) that made the sharp spear.'

48 

Banggala	**birrgalbay**	mirangana	mugina-nggu.
spear	**sharp**	make-PAST	brother-DOER

'Brother made **the sharp spear**.'
(New example) based on SUTTON_P01-001913B (FT)

Putting **banggala birrgalbay** at the start of the sentence emphasises that 'It was the sharp spear that brother made (and not the boomerang).'

While we can have a lot of fun and say a lot of different things when we change the order of words, we must make sure we do a few things:

- That we always put **-nggu** on the end of the doer of the action. If we don't put this word ending on, we don't know who is doing the action and who is receiving it.
- We must always keep the adjective (description word) with the word that it describes (see section 4.8 on adjectives). In the above sentence, this means keeping **banggala** 'spear' and **birrgalbay** 'sharp' together. If we have a sentence with the word 'spear' **banggala** and the word 'boomerang' **wangal** and we jumble the words up completely, we won't know whether **birrgalbay** 'sharp' refers to the spear or the boomerang.

Sentences with only a doer

Sometimes, verbs don't have a *receiver* of the action. Some examples in English would be: 'I slept', 'you arrived' and 'he lied'. Even if you wanted to put a receiver in these sentences, you couldn't. It would sound wrong. For example, you can't say: 'I slept the baby'. It just sounds wrong. The verb 'to sleep' can only talk about the person sleeping.

Some verbs like this in Gudjal are **bundji** 'sleep', **birra** 'talk', **wuni** 'die', **dhanda** 'fall'. In Gudjal, when we have a verb like this, we don't use the **-nggu** ending on the person or animal experiencing or doing the action.

49 

Wuni-na gaygara.
die-PAST kangaroo

'The kangaroo **died.**'/'A kangaroo **died.**'
SUTTON_P01-001913B (FT)

50 

Bulari mugina **bundji-li.**
Two brother **sleep-CONT**

'Two brothers **are sleeping.**'/'The two brothers **are sleeping.**'
SUTTON_P01-001912A (RP)

In the two examples above, 'the kangaroo' and 'the two brothers' are the subjects. Verbs that do not take a receiver are called '*intransitive*'. Verbs that ***must*** have both a doer and a receiver are called '*transitive*'. See section 5.1 on page 39 and 40 for a list of some transitive and intransitive verbs.

Careful!

Whether we use **-nggu** or not depends on the verb we use. Some verbs, like **gandji** 'take', for example, always have a doer and a receiver. You can't just say 'I took'. It would sound wrong. We must use the ending **-nggu** on the doer of this action, even if we don't name a receiver. It's because the receiver is implied.

For example, Freddie Toomba was having a conversation about someone's mother. He says, 'A man took (her)'.

51 

Yarala-nggu gandji-na.
man-DOER take-PAST

'A man took (her).'/'**A man took off** (with her).'
SUTTON_P01-001913B (FT)

He doesn't use the word **yanga** 'her' because both speakers are already talking about her. This means the sentence doesn't have a receiver. But because he used the verb **gandjina** 'took', which always has a doer and a receiver, he had to indicate the doer by adding the doer ending **-nggu** on **yarala** 'man'.

Doer pronouns

We've seen how words like 'kangaroo', 'brother' and 'dog' take **-nggu** when they are the doer of a transitive verb. But pronouns never take **-nggu**. (Remember, pronouns are words like **ngaya** 'I').

If we want to use a pronoun and show that someone is a doer of an action, we use a doer pronoun.

Talking about ourselves:

'I'	**ngaya**
'we two'	**ngali**
'we all'	**nganha**

52

Hear all the doer pronouns.

Talking about the person we're speaking to:

'you' (one person)	**yinda**
'you two'	**yubala**
'you lot' (more than two)	**yura**

Talking about other people:

'he/her/it'	**nhula**
'they two'	**bula**
'they all' (more than two)	**dhanha**

We can use doer pronouns with every verb. It doesn't matter whether it has a receiver or not.

53 

Gaygara-wu	**yani-yngga**	**ngaya.**
kangaroo-TO/FOR	**go-MIGHT**	I

'**I'm going out** for a kangaroo.'/'**I will go** for the kangaroo.'

SUTTON_P01-001913B (FT)

54 

Dhanha	**yani-na.**
They	**go-PAST**

'They **went**.'

(New example)

Receiver pronouns

If we want to say someone receives an action (e.g. 'he hit me'), we use a receiver pronoun. The pronoun in black comes from Gudjal, and the rest come from Warrongo.

55 

Hear all the receiver pronouns.

Talking about ourselves:

'me'	**ngana**
'us two'	**ngalinya**
'all of us'	**ngananya**

Talking about the person we're speaking to:

'you'	**yina**
'you two'	**yubalanya**
'you lot' (more than two)	**yurranya**

Talking about other people:

'him/her/it'	**nyunya**
'them two'	**bulanya**
'them lot' (more than two)	**djananya**

Here's an example of a receiver pronoun:

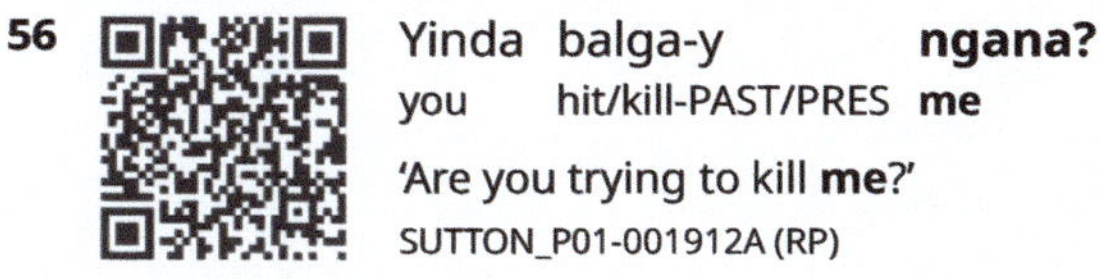

56 Yinda balga-y **ngana?**
you hit/kill-PAST/PRES **me**
'Are you trying to kill **me**?'
SUTTON_P01-001912A (RP)

4.8 Adjectives, describing words

Adjectives (describing words) in Gudjal work in very similar ways to nouns (words for people, places or things). The main difference is that in Gudjal sentences, adjectives mostly come *after* nouns.

57 

Djina **warul / warulgaram**
foot **big**

'big foot'/'The foot is **big**.'
SUTTON_P01-001913A (FT)

Note: The word for 'big' can be either **warul** or **warulgaram**.

As we will see later, we don't use the word 'is' in Gudjal, so the above example can also mean 'the foot is big'.

58 Galamu-galamu **warngura.**
old person **woman**
'(She is) an old **woman**.'/'The old person is **a woman**.'/
'The old person is **female**.'
SUTTON_P01-001913A (FT)

You might be wondering why the word meaning 'old' comes before the word meaning 'woman'. We think that **warngura** 'woman' is the adjective in this example. So, it can be read as 'a female old person'.

59 

Djumbi **gulgandjarra.**
tail **long**
'(It is) a **long** tail.'/'The tail is **long**.'
SUTTON_P01-001913A (FT)

60 

Waybala walwa-**ngan.**
white man **no good-###**
'(He is) a **no good** white man.'/'The white man is **no good**.'
SUTTON_P01-001912A (RP)

It is more common for adjectives to come after nouns, as in this example.

61 

Gadha **balnggarri.**
head **bald**
'(It is) a **bald** head.'/'The head is **bald**.'
TSUNODA_T08-003412B (HB)

However, adjectives can also sometimes come before nouns, as in this example.

62 

Balnggarri gadha.
Bald head
'(It is) a **bald** head.'/'The **bald** (thing) is a head.'
TSUNODA_T08-003412B (HB)

Combining nouns, adjectives and word endings

Adjectives and nouns are very similar in Gudjal, and can both take the same endings.

When you put a noun and an adjective together, and you want to add a word ending, you add the ending to the *last* word of the pair, no matter whether we see it as more like a noun (a person, place or thing) or more like an adjective (a describing word). For **galbiri dharibara**, it would be:

63 

galbiri **dharibara-wu**
kid **good-TO/FOR**
'**for** the good kid'/'**to** the good kid'
(New example) based on Gugu-Badhun, Sutton 1973, p 99

64 

Yarala **wubidjay-ngu** wangal.
man **young-POSS** boomerang
'(It is) the young man**'s** boomerang.'/
'The boomerang **belongs to** the young man.'/
'The young man **has** a boomerang.'
(New example) based on Gugu-Badhun, Sutton 1973, p 99

Careful!

We *must* add the word ending to the final word in the phrase, but we can also add the word before it, too, so that both words have the noun ending.

[NO AUDIO AVAILABLE]

. . . nguna-ngumay	**burgil-ngumay**
. . . that-FROM	**billy can-from**

'. . . out of that billy can' / '. . . from that billy can'

Gugu-Badhun, Sutton 1973, p 121

4.9 'Here', 'there', 'this' and 'that'

To say 'here' and 'this', we use the word **yaru**.

65

Yaru	ngaygu	yamba.
this	my	camp/home

'**This** is my home.'

(New example)

Yaru can take endings like other nouns.

66 

Yaru-ngga	nyina-ya.
here-LOC	sit down-ORDER

'Sit down **here**!'

SUTTON_P01-001913B (FT)

67 

Gara	**yara-mundu.**
not	**here-FROM**

'(They're) not **from here**.'

SUTTON_P01-001913B (FT)

Careful!

When you attach the **-mundu** ending to **yaru**, it becomes **yaramundu**, not **yarumundu**, as we would expect.

To say 'there' or 'that', we can say either **nguni** or **nguna**. However, **nguna** usually means 'that' and **nguni** usually means 'there'.

68 

Nguna balga-ya irriyal.
that hit-ORDER tree

'Hit **that** tree (with your spear)!'/'**That one**! Hit the tree!'/'Hit **that**! The tree!'
SUTTON_P01-001912A (RP)

69 

Nguni garra barrala yambala-ngga.
there probably down camp/home-LOC

'(She's) probably down **there** at camp.'/'(She) might be down **there**, at home.'
SUTTON_P01-001913A (FT)

Nguni can combine with endings, too.

70 

Nguni-ngga dhana-yngga.
there-LOC stay-MIGHT

'It will stay **there**.'/'(The spear) will probably stay **there**.'/'(He) left (the spear) **there**.'
SUTTON_P01-001913A (FT)

5 Verbs

In this chapter we discuss verbs, words that describe an action or event, and learn how to combine verbs with endings.

5.1 Intransitive and transitive verbs

In section 4.7 on page 33 we learnt that there are two types of verbs that determine whether a sentence requires only a doer (intransitive), or both a doer and a receiver (transitive).

Here are some intransitive verbs (these verbs *only* have a doer):

'go/come'	**yani-**
'sit'	**nyina-**
'fall'	**dhanda-**
'stay/stand'	**dhana-**
'down'	**yinda-**
'rise/ go up'	**waga-**
'walk'	**wanba-**
'tell'	**ngubi-**
'come'	**yandja-**
'die'	**wula-/wuni-**

71 Hear some of the intransitive verbs.

Here are some transitive verbs (these verbs have a doer and a receiver):

'look for'	**yangga-**
'make'	**miranga-**
'see'	**nhaga-**
'carry'	**gandji-/djulba-**
'give'	**guyba-**
'hear'	**ngambi-**
'get/obtain'	**muga-**
'cook'	**wadju-**
'eat'	**gandja-**
'push'	**bubudha-**
'kill'	**guni-**

72 Hear some of the transitive verbs.

(cont.)

'bite'	**badha-**
'break'	**gundji-**
'tell'	**ngubi-**

Note: We think **ngubi-** 'tell' can be both a transitive verb and an intransitive verb.

5.2 How to say 'is'

Gudjal doesn't use words like 'is', 'am', 'are', 'be', etc. Instead, words are put next to each other to show their relationship, with no verb needed in the sentence.

73 

Wandha minggala?
where firestick
'Where **is** the firestick?'
SUTTON_P01-001913A (FT)

74 

Mugina wandha?
brother where
'Where **is** (my) brother?'
SUTTON_P01-001913A (FT)

75 

Ngaygunda birrgalbay.
mine sharp
'Mine **is** sharp.'/'My (spear) **is** sharp.'
SUTTON_P01-001913B (transcript only) (FT)

5.3 Telling someone to do something

We can give orders using verbs in Gudjal just like we can in English. *Sit down! Stop! Look!* These are all orders in English. We don't have to do anything special to the verb when we give orders in English, but in Gudjal we have to add the verb ending **-ya**. You might like to think of this **-ya** as an exclamation mark (!).

76

Guyba-**ya.**
give-**ORDER**
'Give (it)!'
SUTTON_P01-001913B (FT)

77 

Nyina-**ya.**
sit-ORDER
'Sit!'/'Sit down!'/'Have a seat.'
SUTTON_P01-001913A (FT)

Being more specific

If you want to tell someone to do something a bit more specific, like sitting here, or looking at the lightning, then this extra information usually comes *before* the verb.

78

Yaru-ngga	nyina-**ya.**
here-LOC	sit (down)-**ORDER**

'Sit (down) here!'
SUTTON_P01-001913B (FT)

79

Madjala	nhaga-**ya.**
lightning	look (at)-**ORDER**

'Look at the lightning!'
SUTTON_P01-001913A (FT)

'You lot do . . .'

We can also change who we're giving the order to by adding a pronoun to the sentence. Remember that there are lots of ways to say 'you' in Gudjal. If we want to add a particular 'you' to our order (such as 'you two' or 'you lot—'), then we usually put the pronoun at the end of the sentence. We should use our doer pronouns for orders.

80 Hear all the 'you do' pronouns.

'you' (one person)	**yinda**
'you' (two)	**yubala**
'you' (more than two)	**yura**

81

Burila	miranga-**ya**	**yinda.**
fire	make-**ORDER**	**you (one person)**

'**(You)** make a fire!'
SUTTON_P01-001913A (FT)

82

Wungubala-nggu	ngubi-**ya**	**yubala.**
###-DOER	tell-**ORDER**	**you two**

'**You two**, tell (it) to me!'
SUTTON_P01-001913B (FT)

83

Gay-ngal	yani-**ya**	**yura.**
###-TO	come-**ORDER**	**you lot**

'**All you**, come here!'
SUTTON_P01-001913B (FT)

Note: In Warrongo, the **-ngal** word ending means 'to', which is explained more in Tsunoda 2011, p 245.

'Let's do . . .'

We can also say 'let's do' something by using one of the two words for 'we' instead of 'you' at the end of the sentence. The **-ya** ending is still used on the verb.

84 

Hear the two 'we' pronouns.

'we two'	**ngali**
'we all' (more than two)	**nganha**

85 

Yambala-wu	gandji-**ya**	**ngali.**
camp/home-TO/FOR	take/carry-**ORDER**	**we two**

'Let's take it to camp!'/'How about me and you take it to camp?'
SUTTON_P01-001913A (extra transcript) (FT)

86 

Yambala-wu	yani-**ya**	**nganha.**
camp/home-TO/FOR	go-**ORDER**	**we all**

'Let's go home!'/'Let's all go home!'
(New example)

'Don't . . .'

If we want to tell someone not to do something (e.g. 'Don't eat that!'), then we put the word **ngalnga** 'don't' at the start of the order.

87 

Ngalnga	guyba-**ya.**
don't	give-**ORDER**

'**Don't** give (it to them)!'/'**Don't** give!'
SUTTON_P01-001913B (FT)

88 

Ngalnga	gunma-**ya.**
don't	break-**ORDER**

'**Don't** break (it)!'
SUTTON_P01-001912A (RP)

5.4 Talking about the past and the present

Using the same ending for both past and present

In Gudjal, the same ending can be used for the past (e.g. yesterday) and the present (e.g. today). It shows that the action actually happened, or is happening, not that it could happen or will happen. This ending **-n** goes on the verb. A verb without an ending doesn't make sense. It's ungrammatical. We've already seen one verb ending, -**ya**. In Table 4 on page 57, there is a list of all the Gudjal verb endings that we cover.

89 

Waybala **wula-n.**
white man **die-PAST/PRES**
'The white man **died**.'/'The white man **has died**.'/
'The white man **is dying**.'
TSUNODA_T08-003412B (HB)

90 

Nhula **galga-n.**
he **fall-PAST/PRES**
'He **fell**.'/'He **has fallen**.'/'He **is falling**.'
SUTTON_P01-001911B (RP)

91 

Ngana yinda **nhaga-n.**
what you **look-PAST/PRES**
'What **did** you **look** at?'/'What **are** you **looking** at?'
TSUNODA_T08-003412B (HB)

The context tells us whether it's the past (e.g. yesterday) or the present (e.g. right now). But if you really need to show the difference, you can use the Warrongo words **nyila** 'today' and **gundagunda** 'yesterday'.

Other endings for both past and present: -l, -y

By far, **-n** is the most common word ending that speakers used to talk about the past and present. But this ending can also be **-l** or **-y**, depending on the verb you use. You will mainly see **-l** or **-y** in Gugu-Badhun and Warrongo, but Ranji Pope and Harry Bunn also recorded a few examples of these variations in Gudjal, as well.

92 

Yinda **balga-y** ngana?
you **hit/kill-PAST/PRES** me
'**Are** you **trying to kill** me?'
SUTTON_P01-001912A (RP)

[NO AUDIO AVAILABLE]

Ngana yinda **bida-l?**
what you **eat-PAST/PRES**
'What **did** you **eat?**'
SUTTON_P01-001912A (RP)

[NO AUDIO AVAILABLE]

Ngana yinda **djundjula-y?**
what you **look-PAST/PRES**
'What **are** you **looking at?**'
SUTTON_P01-001912A (RP)

[NO AUDIO AVAILABLE]

Gandu **wula-y.**
dog **die-PAST/PRES**
'(My) dog **died**.'
TSUNODA_T08-003412B (HB)

Using a different ending for the past: -na

You can also use a separate ending to talk about events that happened in the past. Freddie Toomba used the **-na** ending in these examples.

93 

Wuni-na gaygara.
die-PAST kangaroo
'The kangaroo **died**.'/'A kangaroo **has died**.'
SUTTON_P01-001913B (FT)

94 

Yanga-wu garra **yani-na.**
mother-TO/FOR maybe **go-PAST**
'He probably **went** (looking) for his mother.'/
'He has probably **gone** (looking) for his mother.'
SUTTON_P01-001913A (FT)

95 

Yarala-nggu **gandji-na.**
man-DOER **take-PAST**
'A man **took** (her/it/them).'/'A man **carried** (her/it/them).'
SUTTON_P01-001913B (FT)

96 

Yara **yani-na** gani.
man **go-PAST** far
'The man **went** far away.'/'The man **has gone** far away.'
SUTTON_P01-001913A (FT)

In the word **yanina** (went), the 'i' vowel sounds long, 'yaniiina'. We don't have many other examples of long vowel sounds in Gudjal, so for now we will write the word with one 'i'. But remember, when you see **yani** and **-na** together, the 'i' sound is a bit longer.

Using a different ending for the present: -ya

To say that something is happening now and hasn't finished, the ending **-ya** goes on the end of the verb. This is similar to the '-ing' and '-s' endings in English. Freddie Toomba used the **-ya** ending in these examples.

97 

Gabari **dhanda-ya.**
rain **fall-PRES**
'Rain **is falling**.'/'Rain **falls**.'
SUTTON_P01-001913A (FT)

98 

Gari **yinda-ya** guwa.
sun **set-PRES** west
'The sun **sets** in the west.'/'The sun **is setting** in the west.'
SUTTON_P01-001913B (FT)

Notice how, in English, there is a difference between the '-s' ending 'the sun sets' and the '-ing' ending 'the sun is setting?' If I say 'he runs', I mean that he runs regularly, maybe every morning. But if I say 'he is running', I mean that he is running *right now*, as we speak.

The **-ya** ending is used for both meanings in Gudjal. Often, we can work out the exact meaning through context. In the following example, **-ya** means right now. 'Why are you coming?'

99 

Ngani-wu **yani-ya** yinda?
what-TO/FOR **come-PRES** you
'What are you **coming** for?'/'Why are you **coming**?'
SUTTON_P01-001913B (FT)

In the following example, in the first translation sentence **-ya** means generally, or every day. The sun rises every day.

100 

Garila **waga-ya.**
sun **rise-PRES**
'The sun rises.'/'The sun is rising.'
SUTTON_P01-001913B (FT)

Careful!

In English, we only use the '-s' ending when we're talking about someone else. We don't use it when we talk about you or me (e.g. 'the dog runs' is right, but 'I runs' is wrong). However, this isn't the case in Gudjal. The **-ya**, **-na** and **-n** endings can be used for everyone and everything in Gudjal; it doesn't matter whether we're talking about you, me, him, her, us, etc.

Careful!

Remember, we can use **-ya** for right now (e.g. 'he sits down') *and* for orders (e.g. 'sit down!'). We can work out the meaning through context.

5.5 Continuous actions

We can refer to continuous actions (e.g. is running, will be singing, was talking) with the ending **-li**. Continuous refers to actions that take time and don't have a set end point.

101 

Ngaya bulari mugina **bundji-li.**
my two brother **sleep-CONT**

'My two brothers **are sleeping**.'
SUTTON_P01-001912A (RP)

[NO AUDIO AVAILABLE]

Ngalnga **birra-li.**
don't talk-CONT

'(They) aren't **talking**.'
SUTTON_P01-001912A (RP)

Note: You might be wondering why they used **ngalnga** here if it isn't an order. We talk about this in section 5.8, on page 49.

In the recordings, Freddie Toomba often put **-nda** before **-li**. In Warrongo, **-nda** means that an action is repeated several times. If you want to speak more like Freddie Toomba, you might like to say **-nda-li** for continuous, repeated actions, instead of just **-li.**

[NO AUDIO AVAILABLE]

Guni-nda-li gadjira ngalingu.
kill-REP-CONT possum for us two

'**He is killing** the possum for the two of us.'
SUTTON_P01-001913A (FT)

102 

Gandura-nggu **badha-nda-li** yarala.
dog-DOER **bite-REP-CONT** man

'The dog **is biting** the man.'
SUTTON_P01-001913A (FT)

You can also use the **-li** ending when telling someone to do something (see section 5.5, page 45).

[NO AUDIO AVAILABLE]

Nguna **bubudha-li-ya** yinda gadjira-wu.
that **push-CONT-ORDER** you possum-FOR

'**Shake** that tree for that possum.'
SUTTON_P01-001913A (FT)

Note that **bubudha-** by itself means 'push', but when we put **-li** on the end it means 'shake', because shaking is like continuously pushing something.

We don't know how to say 'was doing something' in Gudjal, but it might be like this Gugu-Badhun example.

103 

Nhula **wudja-li-n**
he **eat-CONT-PAST**

'He **was eating** (it).'
(Gugu-Badhun) Sutton 1973, p 148

Careful!

In Gugu-Badhun, the **-n** ending only means past, not the past and present together as it does in Gudjal.

5.6 Talking about the future

There are two main ways to talk about the future in Gudjal. One is with the ending **-gu** and the other is with the ending **-yngga**. Let's look at when to use each of these.

'I intend to do . . .'

To talk about our intentions or plans, the verb ending **-gu** is used. For example, think about the sentence 'I plan to walk the dog.' When someone says this, do we think about them walking the dog *yesterday*? Do we think they're walking the dog *right now*? Not really. Generally, we think they're going to walk the dog in the future (whether that be later that day, or another time further in the future). You might like to think of this ending as an 'intend to' or even 'want to'.

104 **Yani-gu** yamba-wu.
go-WILL home-TO/FOR
'(I'm) **going** home!'/'(I) **intend to go** home.'
TSUNODA_T08-003412B (HB)

105 Ngaya yagan **yani-gu** birrgu-wu.
I ### **go-WILL** sweetheart-TO/FOR
'I'm **going** walkabout (looking) for a woman.'/
'I'm **going to go** out (looking) for a lady!'
TSUNODA_T08-003412B (HB)

106 Guna **yangga-li-gu** ngaya.
poo **search for-CONT-WILL** I
'I'm **going to** the toilet!'/'I'm **going to go looking** for a toilet.'
TSUNODA_T08-003412B HB

'It might happen'

When something isn't on purpose, or we think something might happen, we generally use the verb ending **-yngga.** We see this ending used a lot with the verb *to fall* (because nobody *plans* to fall over). We also see this verb ending used to describe objects (because they can't make decisions and therefore they can't *plan* to do something). You might like to think of **-yngga** as 'will' or 'could'.

Note that the 'y' in **yani-yngga** isn't really pronounced when it follows 'i' (see example sentences 15 and 47). The 'y' is only pronounced when it follows 'a' and it sounds like the 'ay' in English 'd<u>ay</u>'.

107 

Nguni-ngga banggala **dhana-yngga.**
there-LOC spear **stay-MIGHT**

'The spear **will stay** there.'/'The spear **could stay** there.'
SUTTON_P01-001913B (FT)

108 

Gabari **dhanda-yngga.**
rain/water **fall-MIGHT**

'Rain **will fall**.'/'Rain **might fall**.'/'Water **could fall**.'
SUTTON_P01-001913A (FT)

'I've decided to . . .'

Another way of talking about the future is to use the **-n** ending. You can use this if the future event is very soon and certain. For example:

109 

Ngaya **nyina-n** yamba-wu.
I **sit-PAST/PRES** home-TO/FOR

'(I have decided that) I'm **staying** home.'/'I'm **sitting** in my house.'/
'I **sat** at home.'/'I **am** at home.'
TSUNODA_T08-003412B (HB)

Note: Sometimes speakers used the **-wu** ending to say 'at'. We talked about this in section 4.5, 'More information' on page 28.

5.7 'So that . . . ', 'in order to'

The verb ending **-nyu** is another way of talking about what you intend to do.

110 

Warngura-wu **nhaga-nyu** ngaya.
woman-TO/FOR **look-REASON** I

'I'm **looking** for a woman.'/'I'm **going to look** for a woman.'
SUTTON_P01-001913B (FT)

111 

Gadjira-wu **yangga-nyu** ngali.
possum-TO/FOR **search-REASON** we

'We two **will look for** a possum.'/'We're **going to search** for a possum.'
SUTTON_P01-001913A (FT)

However, **-nyu** is also used to say **in order to** or **to**, as in these sentences:

> 'I'm going home to rest.'
> 'I'm calling the library in order *to* see if they have a new book.'

It usually comes up in sentences with two verbs, and we put it on the second verb.

112 

Yarala	gani-mundu	wanba-nda-li	wungubala	**birra-nyu.**
men	far-FROM	walk-REP-CONT	###	**talk-REASON**

'The men (have) come a long way **to talk** language.'
SUTTON_P01-001913A (FT)

Note: Freddie Toomba said the above example at the start of his interview with linguist Peter Sutton.

113 

Ngaya	yani-gu	yambala-wu	**nhaga-nyu**	ngaygu	yanga.
I	go-WILL	home-TO/FOR	**see-REASON**	my	mum

'I'm going home **to see** my mum.'/'I'm going home **in order to see** my mum.'
(New example)

5.8 Saying something didn't happen: 'not', 'don't'

'Not'

Gara means 'not' (or 'did not', 'will not', 'don't', etc.) and it comes at the start of the sentence.

114 

Gara	yara-mundu.
not	here-FROM

'You lot **are not** from here.'
SUTTON_P01-001913B (FT)

[NO AUDIO AVAILABLE]

Gara	nhaga-y
not	see-PAST/PRES

'I **don't** see.'
BREEN_G13-001889B (GR)

'Don't'

You may remember that **ngalnga** means 'don't' when we're giving orders (e.g. 'don't do that!'). Sometimes speakers also used **ngalnga** to mean 'not' or 'don't' for statements, as well as orders, as in the next example. This was rare, though.

[NO AUDIO AVAILABLE]

Ngalnga	birra-li.
Don't	talk-CONT

'(They) **don't** talk.'/'(They) **aren't** talking.'
SUTTON_P01-001912A (RP)

In general, to say 'don't', stick with **gara** for statements and **ngalnga** for orders.

5.9 How to say you don't know something

'Maybe'

To say 'maybe', 'probably', 'could have' or 'must have' in Gudjal, we use the word **garra**.

115 

Yanga-wu	**garra**	yani-na.
mother-TO/FOR	**no**	go-PAST

'He **probably** went to his mother (to ask her something).'/
'He **must have** gone for his mother.'/
'**Maybe** he went (looking) for his mother.'/
'He **could have gone** for his mother, I don't know.'
SUTTON_P01-001913A (FT)

116

Nguni	**garra**	barrala	yamba-ngga
there	**maybe**	down there	camp-LOC

'She's **probably** down there at camp.'/'She **must be** down there at camp.'/
'She **could be** down there at camp, I don't know.'
SUTTON_P01-001913A (FT)

'For some unknown reason'

To say 'for some reason', **garra** comes after a 'wh-' word ('who', 'what', 'when', 'where', 'why', how'; see section 6.1, page 51.). It specifies an unknown person, thing, time, place, reason or way.

117

Ngani-wu	**garra**	yani-na	gani.
what-TO/FOR	**[unknown]**	go-PAST	far

'I **don't know** why he went there.'/'For some **unknown reason** he left.'
SUTTON_P01-001913A (FT)

118

Wanhu-ngu-nda	nguna	**garra.**
who-POSS-###	that	**no**

'**I don't know whose** it is!'/'**I don't know who** it belongs to.'/
'It belongs to **someone**.'
SUTTON_P01-001913B (FT)

119

Ngana	**garra.**
what	**no**

'I **don't** know.'
(New example) based on Gugu-Badhun, Sutton 1973, p 161

Note: We don't have a Gudjal example of 'something' or 'I don't know', but in Gugu-Badhun, it is **ngana gada** ('what no'). The words '**gada**' and '**garra**' are related, so we could use the Gugu-Badhun structure, but replace the '**gada**' with '**garra**'.

6 Other aspects of grammar

In this chapter, we get into some more complex grammar, starting with asking questions.

6.1 Questions

There are two different ways of asking questions in Gudjal. The first way asks for a yes or no answer, and the second way uses open questions to ask for more information.

Yes/no questions

To ask a yes/no question, say the sentence as if you were telling someone, but raise your voice at the end of the sentence. We do this in English. For example, if you read the following sentence out normally, you're telling someone that James wants to go to the movies.

'James wants to go to the movies.'

But if you raise your voice at the end of the sentence, you're asking a question.

'James wants to go to the movies?'

It's the same in Gudjal. The following sentence can be understood as a statement or a question, depending on your intonation.

120 

Gani-mundu	yandja-na	yinda?
far-FROM	come-PAST	you

'Did you come a long way?'/
'You came from a long way away.'
(New example) based on SUTTON_P01-001913A (FT)

'Wh-' questions

A 'wh-' question is formed using a 'wh-' question word (we include 'how' in this list). Here are some of the most common 'wh-' question words and their translations in Gudjal.

'What?'	**ngani/ngana**
'Where?'	**wandha/wandja**
'Who?'	**wanhu/wanyu/ngani**
'Why?/for what?'	**nganiwu**
'How?'	**wandharri**
'When?'	**nganimbarringgu**

121 

Hear all the 'wh-' question words.

NOTES FOR THE READER:

- The words for 'how' and 'when' come from Gugu-Badhun.
- **Wandha** and **wandja** mean the same thing. They just represent small differences between Gudjal speakers.
- **Wanhu** and **wanyu** also mean the same thing. Again, they just represent small differences between Gudjal speakers.
- The 'w' in **nganiwu** is very soft, so the word often sounds like 'nganiu'.

Here are some example 'wh-' questions.

122

Wandha minggala?
where firestick

'**Where**'s the firestick?'
SUTTON_P01-001913A (FT)

123

Ngani yinda nhaga-ya?
what you look-PRES

'**What** are you looking at?'
SUTTON_P01-001911B (RP)

The 'wh-' word is usually placed at the beginning of the sentence, but not always.

124

Mugina **wandha?**
brother **where**

'**Where** is (your) brother?'
SUTTON_P01-001913A (FT)

6.2 Saying 'and' or 'but'

'I washed the dishes and Mary dried them.'

In English, we use words like 'and' or 'but' to show relationships between sentences. Gudjal doesn't have any words like 'and' or 'but' to link sentences together. You just put the sentences next to each other.

125 

Gaygara nhaga-na ngali, yara yani-na mudhara-ngga.
wallaroo see-PAST we man go-PAST scrub-LOC

'We saw a wallaroo, **and** a man went into the scrub (after him).'
SUTTON_P01-001913B (FT)

Notice how there's no word for 'and' in the Gudjal example, but there is in the English translation. If you really want a linking word, you can use the Warrongo word **ngunangumay**, which means 'after that'. In Gudjal, it might have had three forms:

1. **ngunangumay**
2. **ngunangumaya**
3. **ngunamundu**

6.3 Drawing attention to a word

In section 4.7 on page 32, we talked about how putting words at the start of the sentence can make them stand out. It is similar to stressing a word in English. For example: 'Did Mary make this?' 'No, I made it.'

Another way to do this in Gudjal is to add the ending -**giya** after the word you want to stress. For example, if you want to stress that 'I did something' (and *not* someone else), you put **-giya** after the word 'I': **ngaya-giya.**

126 

Manda,	**ngaya-giya**	miranga-na.
no	**I-EMPH**	make-PAST

'No, **I** made (it).'
SUTTON_P01-001913B (FT)

You can also use it after adjectives like 'good' or 'big' to add emphasis:

127 

Wayngu-giya.	Ngalnga	guyba-ya	dhanangu.
bad-EMPH	don't	give-ORDER	to them

'**(Pay attention because they're) bad.** Don't give them anything.'
SUTTON_P01-001913B (FT)

We still need to do more research on this word, and it's possible that it was used in more ways than just adding emphasis. But for now, we can use it to show stress.

6.4 Positions: 'up', 'down', 'behind'

The ending **-mali** means 'on the X side of something'. X is whatever word **-mali** is attached to. For example, following the word for 'high' -**mali** can be used to mean 'up there' or 'on top' (i.e. 'on the high side').

128 

Gadharra	**ngarra-mali.**
possum	**high-SIDE**

'The possum is **up there.**'/'The possum is **up** (the tree).'/
'A possum is **on the top side of** (the tree).'
SUTTON_P01-001911B (RP)

129 

Ngarra-mali muga-ya gunma-ya mayi.
up-side get-ORDER break-ORDER honeycomb

'Get the honeycomb **up there** by breaking it!'/
'Get that **up there**! Break the honeycomb!'

SUTTON_P01-001912A (RP)

You can also say 'backside' (i.e. the body part) with the **-mali** ending. It attaches to (what we assume is) the word for 'behind'.

130 

Nhanira-ngga nyina-ya yinda **gurra-mali.**
ground-LOC sit-ORDER you **behind-SIDE**

'Sit down **on your backside** on the sand!'/
'You sit down **on your behind** on the ground!'

SUTTON_P01-001913A (FT)

The ending **-mali** can only attach to a small group of words. We only have the examples of **gurra** 'behind' and **ngarra** 'high' in Gudjal, but Gugu-Badhun has a lot more of these words that **-mali** can attach to.

'downwards/down there'	**bada(-mali)**
'upwards/high'	**ngarra(-mali)**
'on this side'	**guya(-mali)**
'on the other side'	**yara(-mali)**

Warrongo also has several words which go with **-mali**.

'before'	**ganba(-mali)**
'behind'	**gulma(-mali)**
'below'	**gana(-mali)**

NOTES FOR THE READER:

- We believe that Gugu-Badhun's **bada** may be related to Gudjal **barrala** 'downwards'.
- Warrongo's **gulma** may be related to Gudjal gurra 'behind'.

Here is an example of **-mali** from Gugu-Badhun:

131 

Nhawa, **yara-mali** biru-wu.
no **other-SIDE** river-TO/FOR

'No, **past there**, to the river.'

(Gugu-Badhun) Sutton 1973, p 119

Here is one from Warrongo:

132 

Gulma-mali yani.
behind-SIDE come

'(He) is coming behind (me).'

(Warrongo) Tsunoda 2011, p 668

This ending needs a lot more research, so don't worry if you don't understand it straight away. We have trouble with it too!

North, south, east and west

Gudjal speakers used the terms for north, south, east and west a lot. Here are the Gudjal words for those terms:

gunggarri

guwa **wanggarri**

gulbila

133

Hear all the direction words.

These words work a bit differently from other words. They can't take the **-mali** ending, and they usually can't take the endings that other nouns can take, like the location ending **-ngga.** Location is usually implied.

134 

Gari yinda-ya **guwa.**
sun set-PRES **west**

'The sun sets **in the west.**'

SUTTON_P01-001913B (FT)

However, one ending that they can take is the 'from' ending; for example, **-mundu.**

135 

Gulbila-mundu yura wanba-na?
south-FROM you lot walk-PAST

'Did you lot come **from the south**?'

SUTTON_P01-001913B (FT)

6.5 Adverbs

Adverbs change our verbs in one way or another. In English, they often end with '-ly'. Some examples include: 'quickly', 'happily', 'slowly', 'madly', etc. Adverbs can also tell us *when* something happened. 'Yesterday', for example, is an adverb.

Adverbs don't have any special endings in Gudjal.

We don't have a lot of examples of adverbs in Gudjal, so we don't know if there are any special rules which tell us where to put them. However, because they change our verbs, it's probably a good idea to put them next to the verb.

136 

Ngurri guni-ya yinda.
quick(ly) kill-ORDER you
'Kill him, **quick**!'/'**Quickly**, kill him (the possum)!'
SUTTON_P01-001913A (FT)

Here are some helpful Gudjal words for time. Notice how speakers use the location word ending. You might recognise the word **gari** 'sun' in **garingga**. So **garingga** literally means 'sun-at' and would have a meaning somewhat like 'in the sun' (i.e. during the day). Similarly, **gundangga** literally means 'dark-at' (i.e. 'night time').

'at night'	**gundangga**
'during the day'	**garingga**
'tomorrow'	**garralay**

137 

Hear all the 'time of day' words.

Here are some more useful adverbs from Warrongo.

'more'	**ganan**
'once more /again'	**gana**
'badly/ in a wrong way'	**warra**
'in this way / in that way'	**yama**
'yesterday/ last night'	**gundagunda**
'today/soon'	**nyila**

138 

Hear the useful adverbs from Warrongo.

garingga 'daytime'

7 Word endings and pronouns

This chapter lists all the grammar that we've covered in this guide. It provides tables of endings that go on nouns, endings that go on verbs and endings that go on both nouns and verbs. It then lists the pronouns, grouped by person ('I', 'you', 'she/he/it').

7.1 Endings

Table 3. Noun endings

Gudjal ending	Meaning	Abbreviation	Linguistic term	Page
-giya	adds emphasis to what you are saying	-EMPH	emphatic	53
-mundu/-ngumay(a)	'from'	-FROM	ablative	25
-ngga/-da/-nda/ -ndja/-ba	'at', 'in', 'on' (location)	-LOC	locative	26
-nggu	'using', 'with'	-WITH	instrumental	22
-nggu	doer; actor	-DOER	ergative; agent	34
-ngu	'belongs to' (possession)	-POSS	possessive; genitive	28
-wu/-gu	'to', 'for'	-TO/FOR	dative	23

Table 4. Verb endings

Gudjal ending	Meaning	Abbreviation	Linguistic term	Page
-gu	the action will happen	-WILL	future tense	47
-li	the action continues	-CONT	continuous	45
-n/-y/-l	the action is happening now OR in the past	-PAST/PRES	non-future tense	42
-na	the action happened in the past	-PAST	past tense	44
-nda	the action happens repeatedly	-REP	iterative	46
-nyu	'in order to do something'	-REASON	participle of purpose	48
-ya	gives an order or command	-ORDER	imperative	40
-ya	the action is happening now	-PRES	present tense	44
-yngga	the action might or could happen	-MIGHT	subjunctive	47

Other endings:

Table 5. Other endings

Gudjal ending	Meaning	Abbreviation	Linguistic term	Page
-giya	attention, contrast, emphasis	-EMPH	emphatic	53
-mali	'on the side of'	-SIDE	adverb-forming suffix	53

7.2 Pronouns

Table 6 lists all the different pronouns in Gudjal (and Warrongo). Most of these pronouns, except for the Gudjal *doer* pronouns and a few other exceptions, come from Warrongo. Look at the different parts of chapter 4: Nouns, pronouns, adjectives to see where to use each type of pronoun.

All Gudjal pronouns are in black. All other pronouns come from Warrongo and are coloured in blue.

Table 6. Pronouns

		Doer pronouns (discussed in section 4.7)	Receiver pronouns (discussed in section 4.7)	Possessive pronouns (discussed in section 4.6)	'To' and 'for' pronouns (discussed in section 4.3)	'From' pronouns (discussed in section 4.4)
Talking about ourselves	one person	**ngaya** 'I'	**ngana** 'me'	**ngaygu** 'my'	**ngaygunda** 'to/for me'	**ngaygungumay** 'from me'
	two people	**ngali** 'we two'	**ngalinya** 'us two'	**ngalingu** 'our' (belonging to us two)	**ngalingunku** 'to/for us two'	**ngalingumay** 'from us two'
	more than two people	**nganha** 'we all'	**ngananya** 'all of us'	**nganhangu** 'our' (belonging to all of us)	**nganangunku** 'to/for all of us'	**nganangumay** 'from all of us'
Talking about the person we're speaking to	one person	**yinda** 'you'	**yina** 'you'	**yinu** 'your' (belonging to one person)	**yindana** 'to/for you' (one person)	**yinungumay** 'from you' (one person)
	two people	**yubala** 'you two'	**yubalanya** 'you two'	**yubalangu** 'your' (belonging to you two)	**yubalangunku** 'to/for you two'	**yubalangumay** 'from you two'
	more than two people	**yura** 'you lot'	**yurranya** 'you lot'	**yurrangu** 'your' (belonging to you lot)	**yurrangunku** 'to/for you lot'	**yurrangumay** 'from you lot'
Talking about other people	one person	**nhula** 'he/she/it'	**nyunya** 'him/her/it'	**nyungu** 'his/her/its'	**nyungunku** 'to/for him/her/it'	**nyungungumay** 'from him/her/it'
	two people	**bula** 'those two/they two'	**bulanya** 'them two'	**bulangu** 'their' (belonging to them two)	**bulangunku** 'to/for them two'	**bulangumay** 'from them two'
	more than two people	**dhanha** 'they all'	**djananya** 'them lot'	**djanangu** 'their' (belonging to them lot)	**dhanangu** 'to/for them lot'	**djanangumay** 'from them lot'

8 Gudjal skin system

Hear all the Gudjal skin names.

In this chapter we learn about the Gudjal skin names, how the skin system works and a bit about totems.

8.1 Skins

Gudjal has four sections or skin groups. Male and female members of these groups have slightly different skin names. The terms **Gurrguru, Gurrgila, Wunku** and **Wudhurru** are male skin names. Female skin names have **-aynggan** added to them. Note that the final 'u' sound in the male skin names **Gurrguru** and **Wudhurru** is dropped in the female skin names.

Table 7. Skin names

Male	Female
Gurrguru	Gurrgur**aynggan**
Gurrgila	Gurrgil**aynggan**
Wunku	Wunkur**aynggan**
Wudhurru	Wudhurr**aynggan**

Figure 1. Gudjal skin names showing father and child pairs, mother and child pairs, preferred marriage partners and siblings.

A person's skin group shows their relationship to other people in the community and culture. Skin names can be used as a name, just like a kin term. There are rules about which skin groups a person can and cannot speak with, marry, and trade with. There is an ideal marriage partner for Gudjalbara individuals depending on their skin.

This is how Gudjal people used to work out your skin name:

If the brother is	***Gurrgila***	then the sister is	***Gurrgilaynggan***
If the brother is	***Wudhurru***	then the sister is	***Wudhurraynggan***
If the brother is	***Wunku***	then the sister is	***Wunkuraynggan***
If the brother is	***Gurrguru***	then the sister is	***Gurrguraynggan***

If you go through your father's side, you will always be the same skin as your father's father:

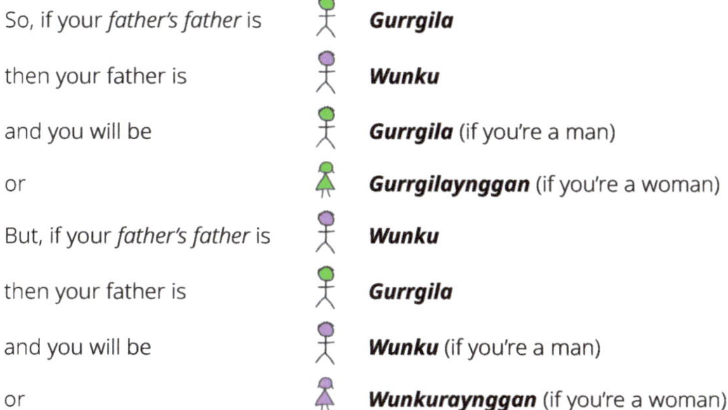

So, if your *father's father* is ***Gurrgila***
then your father is ***Wunku***
and you will be ***Gurrgila*** (if you're a man)
or ***Gurrgilaynggan*** (if you're a woman)
But, if your *father's father* is ***Wunku***
then your father is ***Gurrgila***
and you will be ***Wunku*** (if you're a man)
or ***Wunkuraynggan*** (if you're a woman)

That is one line through the father's side. This is the other line:

If your *father's father* is ***Wudhurru***
then your father is ***Gurrguru***
and you will be ***Wudhurru*** (if you're a man)
or ***Wudhurraynggan*** (if you're a woman)
But, if your *father's father* is ***Gurrguru***
then your father is ***Wudhurru***
and you will be ***Gurrguru*** (if you're a man)
or ***Gurrguraynggan*** (if you're a woman)

If you go through your mother's side, you will always be the same skin as your mother's mother.

So, if your *mother's mother* is ***Gurrgilaynggan***
then your mother is ***Gurrguraynggan***
and you will be ***Gurrgila*** (if you're a man)
or ***Gurrgilaynggan*** (if you're a woman)
But, if your *mother's mother* is ***Gurrguraynggan***
then your mother is ***Gurrgilaynggan***
and you will be ***Gurrguru*** (if you're a man)
or ***Gurrguraynggan*** (if you're a woman)

That is one line through the mother's side. This is the other line:

If your *mother's mother* is ***Wunkuraynggan***
then your mother is ***Wudhurraynggan***
and you will be ***Wunku*** (if you're a man)
or ***Wunkuraynggan*** (if you're a woman)
But, if your *mother's mother* is ***Wudhurraynggan***
then your mother is ***Wunkuraynggan***
and you will be ***Wudhurru*** (if you're a man)
or ***Wudhurraynggan*** (if you're a woman)

For each each group there is one other skin group that is the best one for them to marry. That is called their 'straight skin':

Straight skin for ***Gurrgilaynggan*** is ***Wudhurru***
Straight skin for ***Wudhurraynggan*** is ***Gurrgila***
Straight skin for ***Wunkuraynggan*** is ***Gurrguru***
Straight skin for ***Gurrguraynggan*** is ***Wunku***

The diagram below shows how these skin names apply down the generations, including straight skin marriage partners and children.

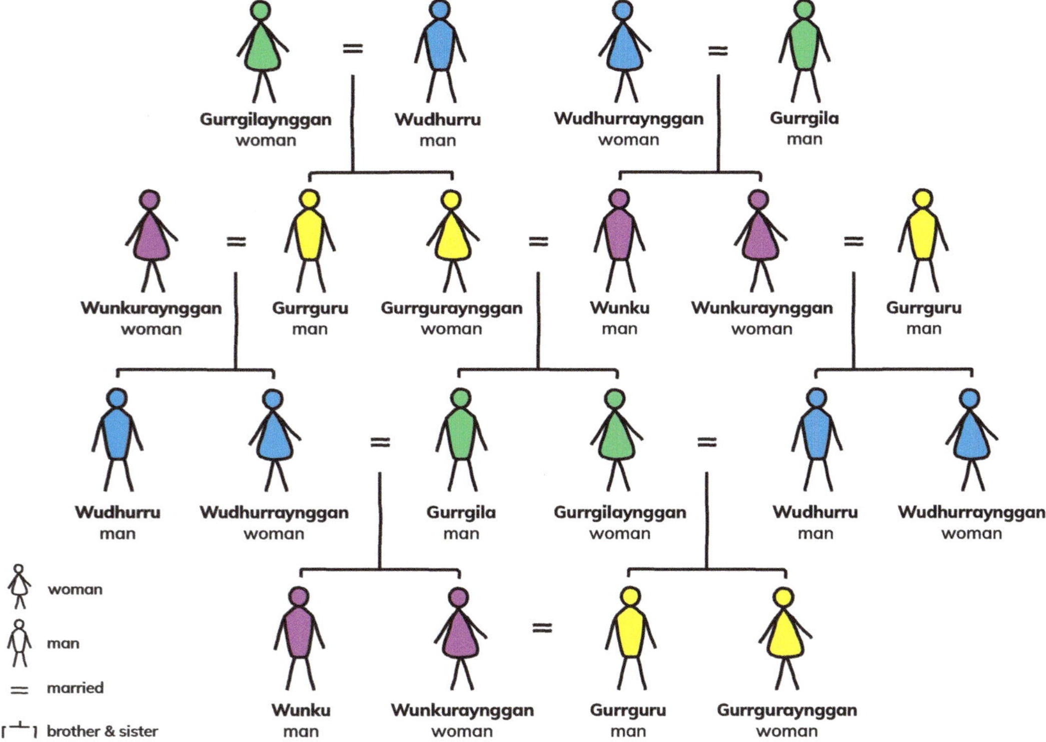

Figure 2. Gudjal skin system as applied to a family tree. By following each of the four skin groups (green, blue, yellow and purple) you can see how the skin names repeat every second generation.

To see how this works in practice, see Figure 3 on the next page which Maggie 'Ton-Ton' Thompson's descendants through her great-grandson William Santo and his descendants. Underlining shows William's direct descendants and ancestors who are Gudjal. This gives you an idea of how skin names are mapped on to kin. The names of individuals are also shown to help you follow the skin system. Try doing one for your own family tree!

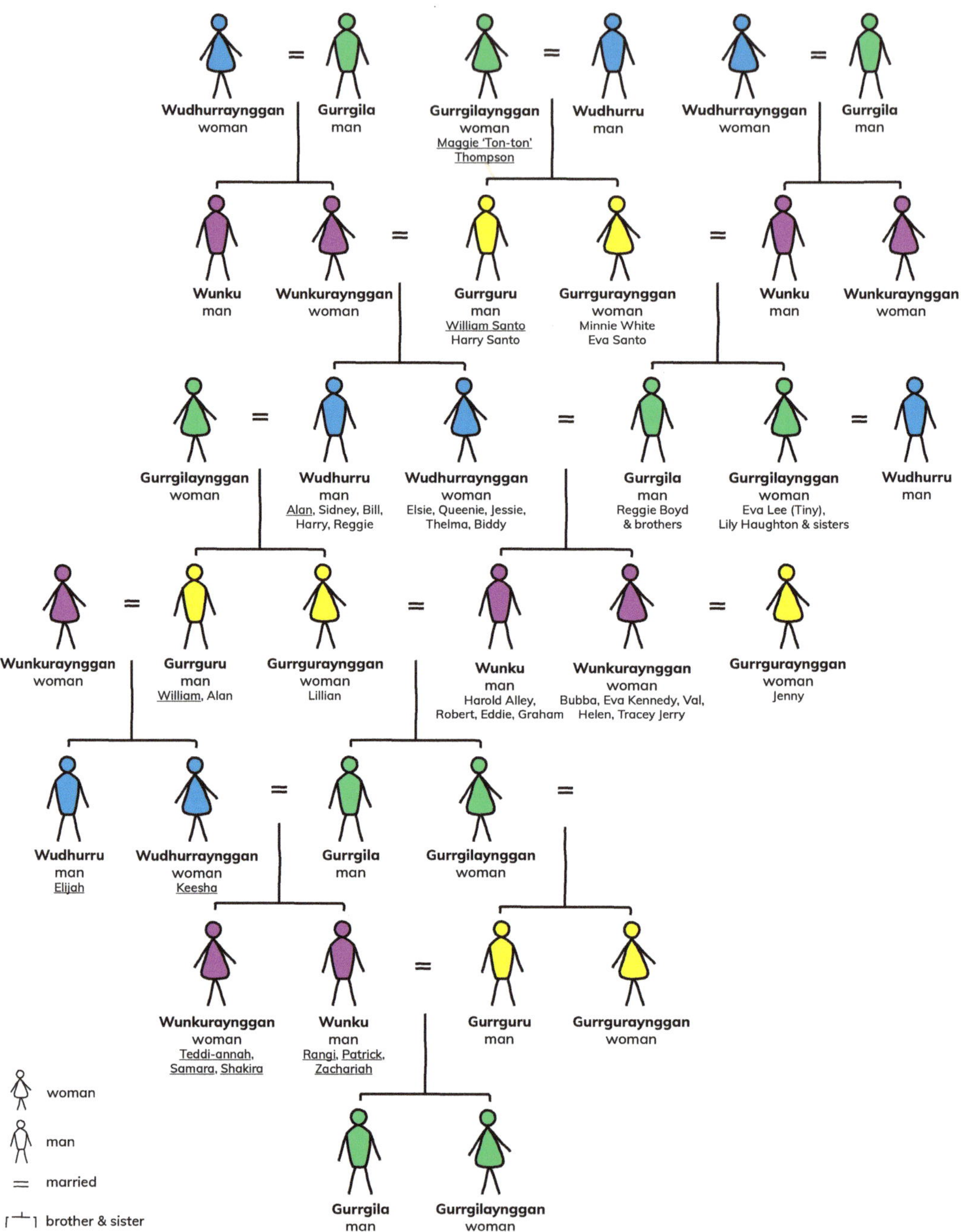

Figure 3. Maggie 'Ton-ton' Thompson's descendants, showing their Gudjal skin names and some names of her descendants through William's line.

8.2 Totems

For a Gudjal person, your totem forms part of your identity. A person's totem may relate to their skin group and the traditional country of their family group. In addition, each person might have their own personal totem that is given through ceremony or by a Gudjal elder. Whereas nation, clan and family totems are predestined, personal totems are given and recognise an individual's strengths and weaknesses. Totems are important, as they link us to the universe, to our land, air, water and geographical features. Each Gudjal person has a responsibility to ensure their totems are protected and passed on to the next generation.

Harry Bunn said that the totem associated with **Gurrguru** skin was **garrgay** 'sparrowhawk' and that the totem associated with **Gurrgila** skin was **guridjala** 'eaglehawk'. He wasn't sure about the others but thought that the totem of **Wunku** skin might be a dove and gave the words **guragay** or **guruga**, which are words we don't know and so are not in this book. He also thought that the totem of **Wudhurru** skin might be **gundulu** 'emu'. Peter Sutton's notes on Gugu-Badhan have the totem associated with **Wudhurru** skin as **guridjala** 'eaglehawk'.

In addition to personal totems, and totems associated with skin names, the Gudjal Nation as a whole is associated with **gundulu** 'emu'.

9 Songs and Welcome

This chapter has four songs which have some Gudjal words in them, the second song is all in Gudjal. There is also Welcome to Country in Gudjal which you can use or modify to create your own versions.

Bayari-
'to sing'

9.1 Songs

Song 1. Gudjalbara

(sung to the tune of 'Hokey Pokey')

140 

William C. Santo

VERSE

C C
You put your dji - na foot in, You put your dji - na foot out, You put your

3 C G G
dji - na foot in, and you shake it all a - bout You do the Gu-djal-ba - ra and you

6 G G C
turn your ba - na - 'round Ya - ni - ya nga - li yuwu!

CHORUS

9 C C C G
Ohh Gu-djal - ba - ra Ohh Gu-djal - ba - ra

13 C F G C
Ohh Gu-djal - ba - ra Ya - ni - ya nga - li yuwu!

VERSE 1
You put your **marndila** in
You put your **marndila** out
You put your **marndila** in
And you **bilba** all about
You do the **Gudjalbara**
And you turn your **bana** around
Yaniya ngali yuwu!

VERSE 2
You put your **mugura** in
You put your **mugura** out
You put your **mugura** in
And you **bilba** all about
You do the **Gudjalbara**
And you turn your **bana** around
Yaniya ngali yuwu!

VERSE 3
You put your **wanban** in
You put your **wanban** out
You put your **wanban** in
And you **bilba** all about
You do the **Gudjalbara**
And you turn your **bana** around
Yaniya ngali yuwu!

VERSE 4
You put your **gurra-mali** in
You put your **gurra-mali** out
You put your **gurra-mali** in
And you **bilba** all about
You do the **Gudjalbara**
And you turn your **bana** around
Yaniya ngali yuwu!

VERSE 5
You put your **bamba warul** in
You put your **bamba warul** out
You put your **bamba warul** in
And you **bilba** all about
You do the **Gudjalbara**
And you turn your **bana** around
Yaniya ngali yuwu!

This song includes the following Gudjal words and phrases:

djina 'foot'

bilba the meaning of this word isn't clear; we are using it here to mean 'shake'

Gudjalbara 'Gudjal people'

bana 'body'

Yaniya ngali yuwu! 'Let's go, yes!'

marndila 'hand'

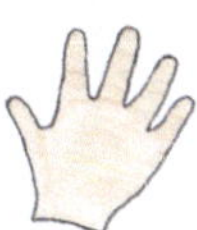

mugurra 'thigh'

wanban 'head'

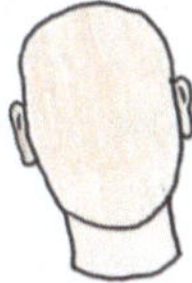

gurra-mali 'backside'

bamba warul 'big belly'

Song 2. Gundulu Galbin

(sung to the tune of 'Hush Little Baby')

141 

VERSE 2
Gundulu galbin **marrgabala**
Gungarri nyila yani-na
Gundulu gaya 'yandja-ya' birra-na
Gudbara-giya yamba yandja-na.

VERSE 3
Gundulu galbin **gudbara**
Gungarri nyila yani-na
Gundulu gaya 'yandja-ya' birra-na
Bulari-giya yamba yandja-na.

VERSE 4
Gundulu galbin **bulari**
Gungarri nyila yani-na
Gundulu gaya 'yandja-ya' birra-na
Nyunkul-giya yamba yandja-na.

This song includes the following Gudjal words and phrases:

birrana 'said'

bulari 'two'

-giya '(adds emphasis)'

gudbara 'three'

gundulu galbin 'baby emu'

gundulu gaya 'father emu'

gunggarri yanina 'went north'

guybaguyba 'big mob'

marrgabala 'four'

nyila 'today'

nyunkul 'one'

yamba yandjana 'came home'

yanina 'went'

yandjaya 'come on'
(Note: this word sounds more like **yindji** in the recording as we weren't sure of the correct pronunciation when it was recorded)

You can see an animated video clip of this song here.

Song 3. Bunba-ngga*

'In the sand'

142 

♩ = 120 VERSE

Am G F
In the begin-ing of the dream-time peo - ple When you hear the Corrob-

4 G Am G F
- oree roar You can see the camp - fire glow-ing And the myths of le-

8 G Am G F
- gends told They lived a heal - thy and quiet life Be-fore the white

12 G Am G F
man came They used their skills for sur-vi - val Now they're just

16 G Am G F G
mem-ories of old What-ev - er hap - pened to yam-ba dha-ri ba-ra-wu

CHORUS

21 Am G F G Am
What-ev - er hap - pened to dhu-la bu-la-ri-wu What-ev - er hap-

26 G F G F G Am
- pened to yi - gi yi-gi-wu Ga-na - ma - li bun-ba-ngga

32 F G Am
Ga-na - ma - li bun - ba - ngga

* **Bunba** 'sand, ashes, dirt' and **-ngga** 'in'.

VERSE 2

Now the dole queues are getting bigger all the time

The young men is waiting for their dole cheques to arrive

The smiles of an old man and his wife are gone

They remember a once-proud race of people oh yeah

Now they see domestic violence, alcohol

Brought on by the society we live in today.

This song includes the following Gudjal words:

yamba 'place', **dharibara-wu** 'good-to'
lit. 'to the good place'

dhula 'sticks', **bulari-wu** 'two-to'
lit. 'to the two sticks'

The word **yigi-yigi** was used across northern Queensland up until the late 19th century for a didjeridu-like instrument.

yigi-yigi-wu 'didjeridu-to' lit. 'to/for the didjeridu'

Gana-mali is neighbouring Warrongo for 'underneath'. No word meaning 'under' was documented in Gudjal, though the ending **-mali** 'side' is both Gudjal and Warrongo.

Bunba-ngga means 'in the sand'.

Song 4. Ngaygu mugina

'My brother'

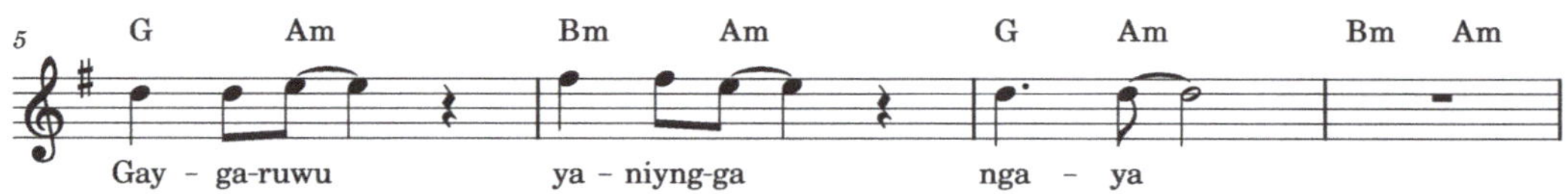

Gaygara-wu	**yani-yngga**	**ngaya**	I'm going for a kangaroo
kangaroo-FOR	go-MIGHT	I	
Gaygara-wu	**yani-yngga**	**ngaya**	I'm going for a kangaroo
kangaroo-FOR	go-MIGHT	I	
Bindamba	**mugina**	**ngurri**	Let go brother, quickly
let go	brother	quick	

9.2 Welcome to Country

144 

1 **Yaru!**
hello
Welcome/Hello

<table>
<tr><td>2</td><td>Ngaya</td><td>Gudjalbara-ngu</td><td>warrngura.</td></tr>
<tr><td></td><td>I</td><td>Gudjal people-of</td><td>woman</td></tr>
</table>

I am an elder/man/woman of the Gudjal people.

<table>
<tr><td>3</td><td>Ngaya</td><td>wandja-na</td><td>ngubi-nyu</td><td>Gudjalbara-ngu</td><td>yambala</td><td>ngani.</td></tr>
<tr><td></td><td>I</td><td>come-PAST</td><td>tell-FOR</td><td>Gudjal people-POSS</td><td>home</td><td>what</td></tr>
</table>

I came to tell you about Gudjalbara country.

<table>
<tr><td>4</td><td>Gudjalbara-ngu</td><td>yambala-ngu</td><td>gunggarri</td><td>nyina-ya</td><td>Gugu-Badhun.</td></tr>
<tr><td></td><td>Gudjal people-POSS</td><td>home-POSS</td><td>north</td><td>sit-PRES</td><td>Gugu-Badhun</td></tr>
</table>

To the north of Gudjal is Gugu-Badhun country.

<table>
<tr><td>5</td><td>Gulbila</td><td>nyina-ya</td><td>Jangga.</td></tr>
<tr><td></td><td>south</td><td>sit-PRES</td><td>Jangga</td></tr>
</table>

To the south is Jangga country.

<table>
<tr><td>6</td><td>Wanggarri</td><td>nyina-ya</td><td>Wulgurukaba, Bindal.</td></tr>
<tr><td></td><td>east</td><td>sit-PRES</td><td>Wulgurukaba Bindal</td></tr>
</table>

To the east is Wulgurukaba and Bindal countries.

<table>
<tr><td>7</td><td>Guwa</td><td>nyina-ya</td><td>Yirandali.</td></tr>
<tr><td></td><td>west</td><td>sit-PRES</td><td>Yirandali</td></tr>
</table>

To the west is Yirandali country.

<table>
<tr><td>8</td><td>Mural</td><td>nyina-ya</td><td>yambala-ngga</td><td>Gudjalbara-ngu.</td></tr>
<tr><td></td><td>CT</td><td>sit-PRES</td><td>home-LOC</td><td>Gudjal people-POSS</td></tr>
</table>

Charters Towers sits on Gudjal Country.

<table>
<tr><td>9</td><td>Galamu-galamu yani-na</td><td>yambala-wu</td><td>yunyiman-ngu.</td></tr>
<tr><td></td><td>elders</td><td>go-PAST home-TO</td><td>spirit-POSS</td></tr>
</table>

Elders have gone to the spiritual home.

<table>
<tr><td>10</td><td>Nganha</td><td>djananya</td><td>ngambi-ya.</td></tr>
<tr><td></td><td>we</td><td>them</td><td>hear-PRES</td></tr>
</table>

We listen to them.

<table>
<tr><td>11</td><td>Yaru</td><td>warngura</td><td>yarala</td><td>birra-gu.</td></tr>
<tr><td></td><td>here</td><td>women</td><td>men</td><td>talk-WILL</td></tr>
</table>

Here women and men will talk.

<table>
<tr><td>12</td><td>Nganha</td><td>djananya</td><td>ngambi-ya.</td></tr>
<tr><td></td><td>we</td><td>them</td><td>hear-PRES</td></tr>
</table>

Let's listen to them.

Dictionary

Gubura
'magpie'

10 Gudjal to English dictionary

In this part of the book, we give you three ways of finding Gudjal words. The first is a Gudjal to English dictionary, with Gudjal headwords in alphabetical order. The second is a list of Gudjal words grouped into categories. Here you can find a list of, for example, bird names, or parts of the body. The third part is an English to Gudjal finder list. Let's look at how the dictionary entries are laid out in this chapter.

How to use the dictionary

A dictionary word entry looks like this:

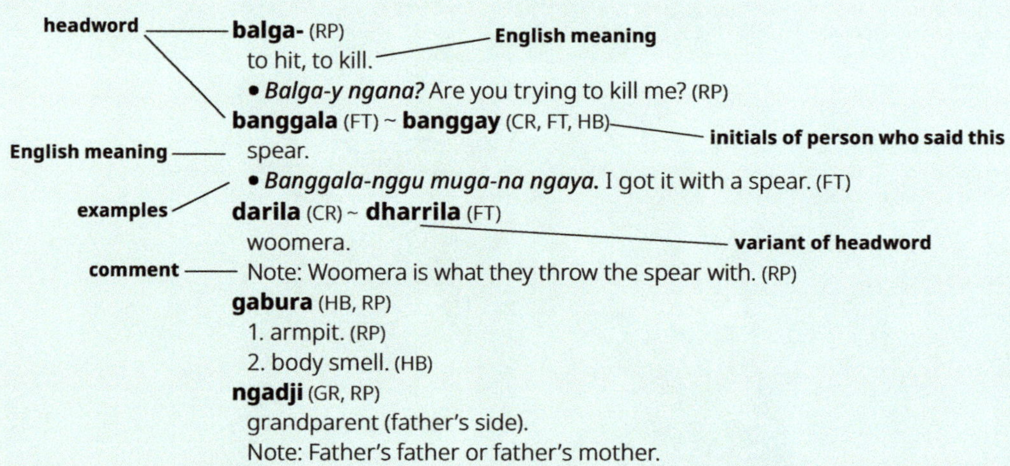

Headword

The entry begins with the Gudjal word in bold. Verbs end in a hyphen, which means they typically need another ending (see Table 4: Verb endings). All other words are nouns, pronouns or adjectives. Sometimes there is a variant of this word, and this is listed after the ~ symbol. The headword is followed by the initials of the person or people who said this word.

English meaning

The meaning of the Gudjal word is given in English. Many words in Gudjal may not have an exact match in English, so there might be a few English meanings given. Some headwords have more than one meaning and these meanings are numbered.

Comments

Sometimes there will be a comment, following the work 'note', that explains where the word has come from or explains the meaning in more detail.

Examples

Some dictionary entries have an example of how the word is used in Gudjal, and a translation into English. These come from Sutton's fieldnotes and Anderson's transcriptions of the Gudjal recordings. Each meaning is followed by the initials of the person or people who gave this English meaning to the Gudjal word, or (NEW), which refers to a new example sentence, one that is in this book but not on the recordings.

The headwords in the dictionary section are ordered alphabetically according to the Gudjal spelling system, thus: b, d, dh, dj, g, i, m, n, ng, nh, ny, r, w, y.

Abbreviations used in the dictionary

BD	Bluff Downs — referring to a wordlist created by EED White of Bluff Downs, circa 1919
CR	Clarke River — referring to a wordlist created by Gresley Lukin at Clarke River in 1886
FT	Freddie Toomba
GR	George Reid
HB	Harry Bunn
HS	Homestead — referring to a wordlist created by Archibald Meston at Homestead, circa 1900
RP	Ranji Pope
WS	William Santo

B b

badha- (FT)
bite.
• *Gandura-nggu badha-nda-li yarala.* The dog bites the man. (FT)

badhara (GR)
wallaby.

badhu (RP)
woman's private parts.

badji (RP)
full.

badjuru (WS)
money.

balalbara (BD, FT)
moon.

balanu (CR, HB, HS, RP)
moon.

balbaray (FT)
bone.

balbari (FT)
shin.

balbira (GR) ~ **barrbira** (FT, HB, RP)
porcupine (echidna).

balga- (RP)
to hit, to kill.
• *Balga-y ngana?*
Are you trying to kill me? (RP)

balgadhala (FT)
blood.

balgu (CR, FT, GR, HB, RP)
axe, stone tomahawk.

balnggari (HB)
forehead.
• *Balngarri gadja.* Bald head. (HB)

bama (RP)
Aboriginal man.
• *Bama yani-gu ngalingunda.*
A man is coming towards us. (RP)

bamba (FT, RP)
belly, chest.
• *Bamba warulgaram.* Big belly. (FT)

bambabari (HB)
pelican.

bambu (RP)
egg.

bana (GR, HB, RP)
body, belly, liver.
• *Bana ngaya bundjabirri-ngan manda-wu.*
My belly is very hungry for food. (RP)

bana (GR)
water, rain.

bandara (RP)
weather.

banggarra (GR, RP)
blue-tongue lizard.

banggay (CR, FT, HB) ~ **banggala** (FT)
spear.
• *Banggala-nggu muga-na ngaya.*
I got it with a spear. (FT)
• *Banggay muga-ya.*
Get your spear. (RP)

banggurru (BD, HB, RP)
turtle.

banya (RP)
girl.

baragan (CR)
blood.

bardjala (HB) ~**barrngala** (GR, RP)
kangaroo rat.

bari (CR, FT, HS) ~ **barri** (HB, RP)
stone.
• *Bari baringgalay.* Grey stone. (FT)

baringgalay (FT)
grey.
• *Yarala galamu-galamu baringgalay.*
Old man with grey beard. (FT)

barngan (HB)
kangaroo rat.

barran (HB)
lower arm.

barrbira (FT, HB, RP) ~ **balbirra** (GR)
porcupine (echidna).

barri (HB, RP) ~ **bari** (CR, FT, HS)
stone.
• *Bari baringgalay.*
Grey stone. (FT)

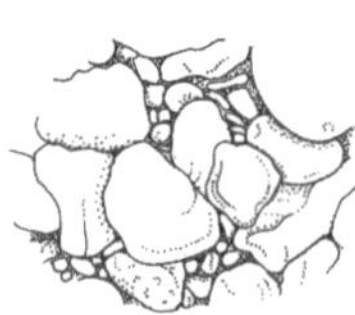

barri (RP)
bone.

bawuru (FT) ~ **bawura** (BD)
rock wallaby.

bayari- (RP)
to sing.
• ***Bayari-gu ngaygunda.***
You'll sing for me. (RP)

baygari (FT)
fig tree.

baylbira (BD)
black bream.

bida- (RP)
to eat.
• ***Ngana yinda bida-l?***
What did you eat? (RP)

bigali- (HB)
to get tired.

bimbala (FT)
hole.
• ***Bimbala warulgara.*** Big mine at Charters Towers. (FT)

bimu (RP)
aunty.
Note: Father's sister or mother's sister.
• ***Guyba-ya-nyu bimu-wu.***
Give it to aunty. (FT)

bina (GR)
ear.

binagari (WS)
deaf.
Note: Not originally in Gudjal language, but has become a shared word among north Queensland Aboriginal languages.

bindamba- (FT)
to let go.
• ***Bindamba!*** Let go! (FT)

bindji (FT)
belly.
Note: From early Australian pidgin.

bindjiri (FT)
frilled lizard.

birra- (RP)
to talk.
• ***Ngalnga birra-li.***
They aren't talking. (RP)

birrbirr (BD)
parrot.

birrgalbay (FT)
sharp.
• ***Mugina-nggu miranga-na banggala birrgalbay.*** My brother made a sharp spear. (FT)

birrgu (BD, FT, HB, RP)
wife (sweetheart).
• ***Birrgu ngaya manda muga-n ngali-ngunda.***
My wife is cooking food for us. (RP)

birri (HB)
close, alongside.
• ***Warngu birri djambal-da djanan.***
The woman is standing alongside a snake. (HB)

birriya (RP)
tongue.

birula (FT)
river.

bubudha- (FT)
to push.

bubudhala (FT)
~ **bubuyal** (FT)
mountain.
• ***Bubudhala-ngga.***
Up in the mountains. (FT)
• ***Bubuyal ngarra.*** High mountain. (FT)

bubudhali- (FT)
to shake.
• ***Nguna bubudha-li-ya yinda gadjirra-wu.***
Shake that (tree) for that possum! (FT)

budhula (GR)
wintertime.

budhulu (GR)
wine.

budja (HB)
woman's private parts.

bugal (HB) ~ **mugal** (HB)
elbow.

bula (RP)
those two.
• *Bula yadimba-ya*. Those two are laughing. (RP)

bulari (HB, HS, RP)
2, two.
• *Garralay miranga bulari.*
Tomorrow I'll make two. (FT)

bulu (GR)
uncle.

bunba (HB, RP)
dust, sand, ashes.

bundji- (RP)
to sleep.
• *Ngaya bulari mugina bundji-li.* My two brothers are sleeping. (RP)

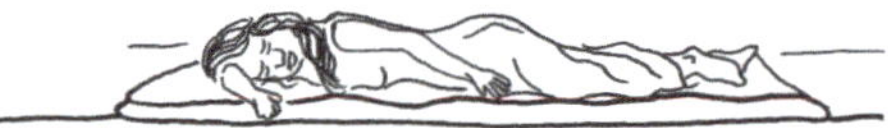

bundjibara (FT)
plum tree.

bundjurru (RP)
boots.

bunga (RP)
penis.

bungguyal (FT)
knee.

bunguy (RP)
fat.

bura (FT)
bora tree.

buri (GR, HB) ~ **burila** (FT)
fire.
• *Burila miranga-ya yinda!* Make a fire! (FT)

D d

dabura (RP)
bad friends, enemies.
• *Ngaya yinda dabura. Yinu-ngan gulibi-ya.*
You and I are bad friends. I am getting wild with you. (RP)

dalay (CR) ~ **dhalan** (GR)
tongue.

dalburu (RP)
fat.

dalimbirri (RP)
yamstick.

dalmbura (HB)
armpit.

dalmbura wangga (HB)
armpit smell.

dambal (RP)
snake (any).

dami (CR) ~ **dhalmira** (FT)
fat.

danguru (GR)
possum.

darila (CR) ~ **dharrila** (FT)
woomera.
Note: Woomera is what they throw the spear with. (RP)

daru (CR)
fire.

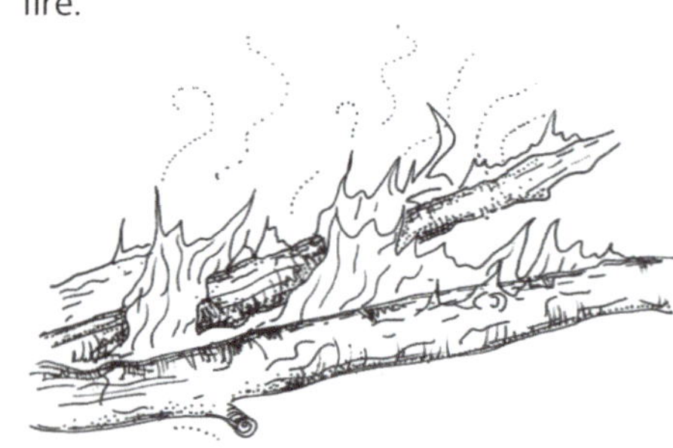

dinggal (RP)
forehead.

dirra (GR) ~ **rirra** (HB, RP)
teeth.

DH dh

dhabu (GR)
cousin.

dhagan (HB, GR) ~ **djagan** (HB)
goanna, bull goanna, spotted one.
Note: This goanna eats dead bullock, so people don't eat it, it's no good. (HB)

dhagay (HB, FT, BD, RP) ~ **djagay** (HB)
goanna, sand goanna.
Note: This is the goanna that people can eat. (HB)

dhalan (GR) ~ **dalay** (CR)
tongue.

dhalbal (RP) ~ **djalbara** (RP)
beard.

dhalmay (BD)
boy.

dhalmira (FT) ~ **dami** (CR)
fat.

dhalmu (FT)
yamstick (fighting stick).
Note: A big yamstick that women fight each other with, a long one. (FT)

dhamarra (RP)
wasp.

dhana- (FT)
to stay.
• ***Nguni-ngga banggala dhana-yngga.***
The spear might stay there. (FT)

dhanda- (FT)
to fall.
• ***Gabari dhanda-ya.*** Rain is falling. (FT)
• ***Gabari dhanda-yngga.*** Rain might fall. (FT)

dhandhari- (FT)
to shake.

dhanga (GR) ~ **djangin** (HB)
tongue.

dhanha (FT)
they.

dharguy (RP) ~ **djarrguyn** (HB)
plains turkey.

dharibara (FT)
good.
• ***Galbirri dharibara.***
Good children. (FT)

dharra (FT, RP) ~ **djarra** (HB)
leg.

dharrila (FT) ~ **darila** (CR)
woomera.
Note: Woomera is what they throw the spear with. (RP)

dharrimu (FT)
woomera.

dhawa (FT, RP) ~ **djawa** (HB)
mouth.

dhili (GR) ~ **djili** (CR, HB, RP)
eye.
• ***Dhili wumbara.*** Sleepy eyes. (GR)

dhina (GR) ~ **djina** (CR, HB, RP)
foot.
• ***Djina warulgaram***. Big foot. (FT)

dhuga (CR, RP) ~ **dhugala** (FT)
smoke.

dhula (GR, RP) ~ **dhulay** (RP)
1. tree.
• ***Nguna balga-ya dhulay.***
(Try to) hit that tree. (RP)
2. stick.

dhulba- (RP)
to jump.
• ***Yinda dhulba-n.*** You jump (into the water). (FT)

dhumba (WS)
sheep.

dhumbi (FT) ~ **djumbi** (HB)
penis, tail.
• ***Dhumbi gulgandjarra.*** Long tail. (FT)
• ***Gaygara-ngu dhumbi.*** Kangaroo tail. (NEW)

dhumuburu (GR, BD, RP)
cattle, bullock, beef.

dhurru (FT, RP)
arm.
• ***Dhurru warul.***
Big arm. (FT)

dinggal (RP)
forehead.

DJ dj

djagan (HB) ~ **dhagan** (HB, GR)
goanna, bull goanna, spotted one.
Note: This goanna eats dead bullock, so people don't eat it, it's no good. (HB)

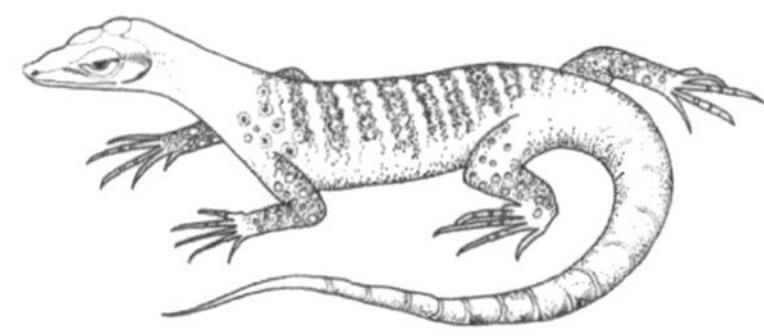

djagay (HB) ~ **dhagay** (HB, FT, BD, RP)
goanna, sand goanna.
Note: This is the goanna that people can eat. (HB)

djalbara (RP) ~ **dhalbal** (RP)
beard.

djalbarayi (HB)
moustache.

djalun (HB)
upper arm.

djamban (RP)
star.

djambu (RP)
tree grub.

djana- (HB)
to stand.
• *Warngu birri djambal-da djanan.* The woman is standing alongside a snake. (HB)

djangin (HB) ~ **dhanga** (GR)
tongue.

djanyi (HB)
face.

djanyin (HB)
eyelash.

djarra (HB) ~ **dharra** (FT, RP)
leg.

djarrguyn (HB) ~ **dharguy** (RP)
plains turkey.

djawa (HB) ~ **dhawa** (FT, RP)
mouth.

djidji- (RP)
to ache.
• *Manu djidji-ngan.* I've got an achy throat. (RP)

djigankara (FT)
willy wagtail.

djili (CR, HB, RP) ~ **dhili** (GR)
eye.
• *Dhili wumbara.*
Sleepy eyes. (GR)

djina (CR, HB, RP) ~ **dhina** (GR)
foot.
• *Djina warulgaram.* Big foot. (FT)

djinaman (RP)
boots.

djinggurang (FT) ~ **djinggu** (CR)
pubic hair.

djirribirri (RP)
woman's private parts.

djumbi (HB) ~ **dhumbi** (FT)
penis, tail.
• *Dhumbi gulgandjarra.* Long tail. (FT)

djundju- (RP)
to look at, to stare at.

G g

gabari (FT)
rain, water.
• *Gabari dhanda-ya.*
Rain is falling. (FT)

gabirri (RP)
emu.

gabu (FT, HB) ~ **gabul** (BD, FT)
snake, carpet snake.

gabura (HB, RP)
1. armpit. (RP)
2. body smell. (HB)

gada (RP) ~ **gadha** (GR, HS)
head.

gadharra (RP) ~ **gadjarra** (CR, FT, GR) ~ **gadjira** (HB)
possum.
• *Ngali yani gadharra-nggu.* You and me are going for possum. (RP)

gadja (GR)
no good.

gadjarra (CR, FT, GR) ~ **gadharra** (RP) ~ **gadjira** (HB)
possum.
• *Ngali yani gadharra-nggu.*
You and I are going for possum. (RP)

gagubara (FT) ~ **gugubarra** (RP)
kookaburra.

galamu (FT)
old (person).
• *Galamu-galamu warngura.*
Old woman. (FT)

galbadhura (FT)
sand.

galbara (RP)
hat.

galbin (CR, FT)
child, baby.
• *Yaru galbin wayngu-giya.*
This kid's no good. (FT)

galbirri (FT, HB, RP)
children.
• *Galbirri wandha?*
Where are the kids? (RP)

galdjara (GR)
children.

galga (GR, RP)
fishing spear (for fish).
• *Yangabara galga.*
Long spear. (RP)

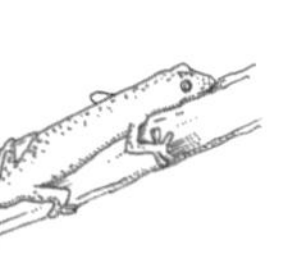

galgan (FT)
ironbark tree.

galmanda (HB)
lizard, small lizard on tree.
Note: Small lizard that climbs up trees. (HB)

galmara (FT, HB, RP)
piss, urine.

galmun (FT)
water.

galun (FT, RP)
testicles.

gambi (RP)
clothes.

gami (GR) ~ **gamiya** (RP)
grandmother.
Note: Mother's mother.

gamu (CR, FT, GR, HS, RP)
1. water. (CR, FT, HS, RP)
• *Yani-nggu gamu-ngga.*
He's gone for a drink of water. (RP)
2. beer. (GR)

ganal (HB)
frog.

gandji- (FT)
to take, to carry.
• *Yarala-nggu gandji-na.*
A man took her. (FT)

gandu (FT, HB, HS, RP) ~ **gandura** (FT)
dog.
• *Gandura-nggu badha-nda-li yarala.* The dog bit the man. (FT)

ganggura (CR)
little.

gani (FT)
far.
• *Yara yani-na gani.*
The man went far away. (FT)

ganibi- (RP)
to go away, to go far away.
gani 'far' plus ***-bi*** 'become'
• *Ganibi-ya!* Go away (a long way)! (RP)

gankari (FT, GR, HB, RP)
knife.

gara (GR, HB) ~ **garra** (RP)
no, don't.
• ***Gara nhagay.*** I don't see. (GR)

gari (FT, HS) ~ **garri** (HB, RP)
sun.
• ***Gari yinda-ya guwa.*** The sun sets in the west. (FT)

garingga (HB, RP)
morning.

garra (FT)
probably, maybe.
• ***Yanga-wu garra yani-na.*** He probably went (looking) for his mother. (FT)

garra (RP) ~ **gara** (GR, HB)
no, don't.
• ***Gara nhagay.*** I don't see. (GR)

garralay (FT)
tomorrow.
• ***Garralay miranga bulari.*** Tomorrow I'll make two. (FT)

garrangandu (RP)
bitter, no good.

Garrgay (HB)
Harry Bunn's totem.

garrgay (HB)
sparrowhawk.

garri (HB, RP) ~ **gari** (FT, HS)
sun.
• ***Gari yinda-ya guwa.***
The sun sets in the west. (FT)

gawa- (RP)
to shout.

gawanda (RP)
belt.

gawaray (FT)
wind.

gawarri (RP)
love.
• ***Bulari gawarri-ngan.***
Two (people) are in love. (RP)

gaya (HB, HS, RP) ~ **gayala** (FT)
father.

gayala (BD, CR)
sun.

gayambula (RP) ~ **gayimbula** (HB)
cockatoo.

gaybal (RP)
1. fire.
• ***Gaybal-du ngaya nyinana.*** I'm sitting next to a fire. (RP)
2. firestick.

gaygara (BD, FT, HS) ~ **gaygarra** (HB, RP)
wallaroo, old man kangaroo.
• ***Gaygara nhaga-na ngali, yara yani-na mudhara-ngga.*** We saw a wallaroo, and a man went into the scrub (after him). (FT)

gayimbula (HB) ~ **gayambula** (RP)
cockatoo.

gayinmadhara- (FT)
to play.

gayu (HB) ~ **gayun** (HS)
Aboriginal woman.

giba (RP)
liver.

gidu (RP)
cold.
• ***Gidu-ngan wuna gamu.***
The water is too cold. (RP)

gigabidi (CR)
mosquito.

ginyu (RP)
baby.

girigira (HB)
guts.

girruwan (HB)
scrub turkey.

giyamara (BD, FT)
white cockatoo.

gubiri (BD, GR, RP)
duck.

gubura (FT)
magpie.

guda (RP) ~ **gudja** (FT, HB)
nose.

gudbara (FT, HS)
3, three.

gudhana (GR) ~ **gudjina** (GR)
sister.

gudhubaya (RP)
pig.

Gudjal (FT, HB)
our language.

Gudjalbari (GR)
our people of Mural (Charters Towers).

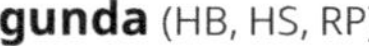

gudjarra (FT)
salt water.

gudjarra (HB)
2, two; or 3, three.

gudjila (HB, RP)
bandicoot.

gudjina (GR) ~ **gudhana** (GR)
sister.

gugara (BD)
bee.

gugubarra (RP) ~ **gagubara** (FT)
kookaburra.

gugudji (HB)
egg.

guguwigan (BD)
girl.

gulbila (FT, HB)
south.
• *Gara gulbila-mundu yura wanbana?*
Did you come from the south? (FT)

gulbuy bama (RP)
old man.

gulgandjarra (FT)
long.
• ***Dhumbi gulgandjarra.***
Long tail. (FT)

guli (FT, RP)
anger, bad temper.

gulibi- (RP)
to get angry.
• ***Yinu-ngan gulibi-ya.***
I am getting wild with you. (RP)

gulmarri (CR, FT)
shield.

gumbugay (HB)
bottom, backside.

guna (HB, RP)
shit, poo.
• ***Guna yangga-li-gu ngaya.***
I'm going to the toilet. (HB)

gunarri (RP)
happy.
• ***Ngalnga gunarri-ngan.*** They're not happy. (RP)

gunda (HB, HS, RP)
dark.
• ***Gunda-ngga.*** Night time. (RP)

gundji- (RP)
to break.

gundulu (BD, CR, FT, GR, HB, HS, RP)
emu.

gunggala (BD)
catfish.

gunggarri (FT, RP)
north.

guni- (FT)
to kill.
• ***Ngurri guni-ya yinda.***
Kill it quickly. (FT)

gunka (HB, RP)
raw.

gunkay (HB)
sunset, gone dark.

gunma- (RP)
to break.
• ***Ngalnga gunma-ya.***
Don't break it. (RP)

gunumali (BD, RP)
brolga.

guridjala (BD)
eaglehawk, wedge-tailed eagle.

gurra (FT)
bottom, backside.
• ***Nhanira-ngga nyina-ya yinda gurra-mali.*** Sit down on your backside on the ground. (FT)

gurralga (HB)
brolga.

gurrbara (BD)
perch.

gurrgalbara (BD)
tree snake.

gurrgarra (RP)
billycan.
• ***Yurra-nggu guyba-y ngaygu nguna gurrgarra?*** What did you put in my billycan? (RP)

Gurrgila (HB)
men's skin name with eaglehawk totem.

Gurrgilaynggan (HB)
women's skin name with eaglehawk totem.

gurrgu (RP)
white.

Gurrguraynggan (HB)
women's skin name with sparrowhawk totem.

Gurrguru (HB)
men's skin name with sparrowhawk totem.

gurrigurri (FT)
hat.

gurrnggal (FT, HB)
husband.

guru (GR)
wind.

gurugay (BD)
female grey kangaroo.

guwa (FT)
west.
• *Gari yinda-ya guwa.* The sun sets in the west. (FT)

guwi (FT)
male ghost.

guwinggan (FT)
female ghost.

guwinggubari (BD)
flying fox.

guyala (FT)
shit.

guyba- (HB)
to give, to put.
• *Ngalnga guyba-ya dhanangu.* Don't give it to them. (FT)

guyba-guyba (FT)
big mob, very many.

guyu (FT, GR, HB, HS, RP) ~ **guyun** (BD)
fish.
• *Wandjabirri guyu-ngan.* He's hungry for fish. (RP)

I i

iliriman (RP) ~ **yiliriman** (RP)
shield.

irriyal (RP) ~ **yirriyal** (RP)
tree.

M m

m

madhira (BD)
burnt grass.

madjala (FT)
lightning.
• *Madjala nhaga-ya!*
Look at the lightning! (FT)

maga (RP)
paint used for corroboree.

mala (CR, GR) ~ **mara** (HB, RP)
hand.
• *Mara-nggu muga-ya manu-ngga.* Get (the bone) out with your hand down your throat. (RP)

malbanani (RP)
dancing grounds.

malgarri (GR)
corroboree.

mambu (FT, HB, RP)
back.

manbabirri (BD, RP)
pelican.

manda (FT)
no.

mandha (FT, HB, RP) ~ **manda** (GR)
vegetable food (bread).
• *Wumay-ngunda manda-ngan.*
The food is sweet. (RP)

manga (HB)
ear.

mangarra (RP)
kangaroo.

manu (FT, HB, RP)
neck, throat.
• *Manu djidji-ngan.*
I've got a sore throat. (RP)

manu ngarra (HB)
nape, back of neck.

mara (HB, RP) ~ **mala** (CR, GR)
hand.
• *Mara-nggu muga-ya manu-ngga.*
Get (the bone) out with your hand down your throat. (RP)

marangan (RP)
this, that.

mari (GR) ~ **marri** (CR, HB)
Aboriginal person.
• *Ngani mari?* Who's that man? (FT)

marndila (FT)
hand.

marrbu (HB, RP)
lice.

marrgabala (FT)
4, four; or several.

marrgid (RP)
gun.
Note: From early Australian pidgin from English 'musket'.

marri (CR, HB) ~ **mari** (GR)
Aboriginal person.
• *Ngani mari?* Who's that man? (FT)

maru (RP)
bone.

mayi (GR, RP)
food.
• *Ngarra-mali muga-ya gunma-ya mayi.*
Climb up there and cut down the honeycomb. (RP)

midin (HB, RP)
possum.

migulu (HB, RP)
white man.
Note: From early Australian pidgin.

milili (FT)
light, blaze.
• *Milili nhaga-na ngaya ngarra, burila-mundu.*
I saw a light up there, coming from a fire. (FT)

mimirri (CR)
wind.

mindjan (HB)
skin.

minga (HB, RP)
woman's private parts.

minggala (FT)
firestick.
• *Wandha minggala?*
Where's the firestick? (FT)

minya (GR, HB, RP)
meat.

miranga- (FT)
to make.
• *Mugina-nggu miranga-na banggala birrgalbay.*
My brother made a sharp spear. (FT)

mirru (FT) ~ **miru** (GR)
club.

mudhara (FT)
scrub, bush.
• *Yara yani-na mudhara-ngga.* A man went into the scrub. (FT)

muga (HS)
4, four; or several.

muga- (RP)
to get, to make, to light.
• *Gaybal muga-ya!* Light the fire! (RP)

mugagan (HB)
lice.

mugal (HB) ~ **bugal** (HB)
elbow.

mugina (FT, RP)
brother.
• *Ngaya bulari mugina bundji-li.*
My two brothers are sleeping. (RP)

mugu (RP)
leg.

mugu (HB)
shoulder.

mugura (FT)
thigh.

munda (GR)
snake (any).

mundja (GR, RP)
tobacco.

mungga (RP)
noise.

mungga- (RP)
to listen.
• *Yadarru, mungga-ya!*
Stop, listen! (RP)

Mural (FT)
name of mountain at Charters Towers.
• *Murul-mundu ngaya.*
I'm from Charters Towers. (NEW)

murray (HB, RP)
hair.

muyu (RP)
bottom, backside.

N n

namba- (RP)
to dance.

nambul (CR)
lips.

nanimbarra (RP)
dirty.

NG ng

n

ngadji (GR, RP)
grandparent (father's side).
Note: Father's father or father's mother.

ngali (FT)
we two.
• ***Yambala-wu gandji-ya ngali.*** Let's us two carry it to camp. (FT)

ngalnga (RP)
not, don't.
Ngalnga gunarri-ngan. They're not happy. (RP)

ngalu (RP)
water.
The word **ngalu** belongs to the coastal tribe and **gamu** is used around Mural (Charters Towers). (RP)
• ***Ngaygundu guyba-ya ngalu.*** Give me a drink of water. (RP)

ngambi- (FT)
to hear.
• ***Nyinggala ngambi-ya!*** Hear the thunder! (FT)

ngamun (FT, GR, HB, RP)
1. breasts. (FT, HB, RP)
2. milk. (GR)

ngana (RP)
what?
• ***Ngana yinda naga-n?*** What are you looking at? (HB)

ngandarri (RP)
small flying insect.
Note: Includes flies, bees, etc. (RP)

ngandharri (FT)
lizard, brown lizard with rough skin.

ngandji (RP)
shoulder.

ngani (RP)
what? who?
• ***Ngani yinda?*** Who are you? (RP)

ngani-mbara (FT)
what kind?

ngani-wu (FT)
why? what for?
• ***Ngani-wu gara yandja-na dhanha.*** Why did they come? (FT)

nganka (FT)
beard.

nganha (FT)
we all.
• ***Yambala-wu yani-ya nganha.*** Let's all go home! (NEW)

nganya (HB)
me.

ngarra (RP)
above, up.
• ***Ngarra-mali muga-ya gunma-ya mayi.*** Climb up there and cut down the honeycomb. (RP)

ngaya (FT, HB)
I.
• ***Ngaya nyina-n yamba-wu.*** I'm staying at home. (HB)

ngaygu
my.
• ***Ngaygu mugina.*** My brothers. (RP)
• ***Yaru ngaygu yamba.*** This is my home. (NEW)

ngaygunda (RP)
to me, for me, myself.
• ***Nhula yani ngaygunda.*** He's coming to me. (RP)

ngayngarra (FT)
cheeky.

ngiduwi- (HB)
to cry.
• ***Galbirri ngiduwi-y.*** That kid is crying. (HB)

ngilan (HB)
girl.

ngubi- (FT)
to tell.

ngulu (RP)
forehead.

nguna (FT) ~ **nguni** (FT)
there, that.
• ***Wanyu-ngunda nguna gara.*** Don't know who that (thing) belongs to. (FT)

ngunmari (RP)
plenty.

ngura- (FT)
to cut.

ngurra (GR, HB)
dingo.

ngurri (FT)
quick, quickly.
• ***Ngurri guni-ya yinda.*** Kill it quickly. (FT)

NH nh

nhaga- (HB, RP)
to see, look.
• *Ngana yinda nhaga-n?* What are you looking at? (HB)
• *Ngaya yani-gu yambala-wu nhaga-nyu ngaygu yanga.* I'm going home to see my mum. (NEW)

nhani (RP) ~ **nhanira** (FT)
ground.
• *Dhanda-yngga yaru nhanira-wu.* He's going to fall on the ground here. (FT)

NY ny

nyina- (HB, RP)
to sit down, to stay.
• *Gaybal-du ngaya nyina-na.* I'm sitting next to a fire. (RP)

nyinggala (FT)
thunder.
• *Nyinggala ngambi-ya!* Hear the thunder! (FT)

nyiri-nyiri (HB, RP)
grasshopper, locust.

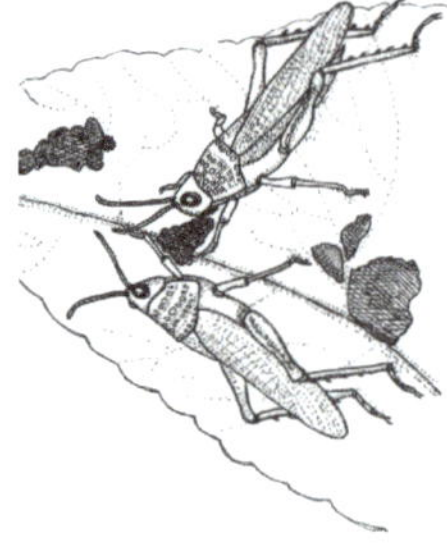

nyunkul (HB, RP) ~ **nyungkaru** (HS)
1, one.

R r

rambu (RP)
thunder.

rirra (HB, RP) ~ **dirra** (GR)
teeth.

rulgu (HB, RP)
heart.

wabagara (BD)
fast, quick.

wadhabara (BD)
quiet bee.

wadhagan (FT, RP) ~ **wadjagan** (HB)
crow.

wadhubara (BD)
hawk.

wadjagan (HB) ~ **wadhagan** (FT, RP)
crow.

waduwingan (RP)
cooked.

waga- (FT)
to rise (of sun).
• ***Garila waga-ya.*** The sun is rising. (FT)

wagal (BD, HB, RP)
eel.

wagwuy (RP)
frog.

walbara (GR)
child.

walmay (BD) ~ **walwa** (HB, RP)
no good, bad, rough.

walu (RP) ~ **walumu** (FT)
ear.

walwa (HB, RP) ~ **walmay** (BD)
no good, bad, rough.
• ***Migulu walwangan.*** The white man is no good. (RP)

wambawuru (HB)
erection.

waminbiri (BD)
good.

wanba- (FT)
to come.
• ***Gulbila-mundu yura wanba-na.*** You come from the south. (FT)

wanban (FT)
head.

wandi (GR, HB, RP)
dingo.

wandjabirri (RP)
greedy, hungry.
• ***Bana ngaya wandjabirri-ngan mandha-wu.*** My belly is very hungry for food. (RP)

wangal (FT, GR, RP)
boomerang.
• ***Wangal gandji-ya.*** Bring your boomerang. (RP)

wanggarri (HB)
east.

wanmalga (FT)
egg.

wanmalga gundulu (FT)
emu egg.

wandha (FT, RP) ~ **wandja** (HB)
where?
• *Wandha minggala?* Where is the firestick? (FT)

wandha-mundu (FT)
where from?
• *Wandha-mundu yinda?* Where are you from? (FT)

wandha-rri (RP)
why? wherefore?
• *Wandha-rri yinda yani?* Why have you come? (RP)

wandha-rru (RP)
where at?

wanyu (FT) ~ **wanhu** (FT)
who?

wanyu-ngunda (FT) ~ **wanhu-ngunda** (FT)
whose?
• *Wanyu-ngunda?* Whose is it? (FT)
• *Wanhu yinda?* What's your name? (NEW)

warbun (CR)
white man.

warngu (GR, RP) ~ **warngura** (FT)
Aboriginal woman.
• *Warngura yanggala ngaya.* I'm looking for a woman. (FT)

waru (BD) ~ **wura** (GR)
kangaroo, big wallaroo.

warul (FT) ~ **warulgaram** (FT)
big.
• *Bamba warulgaram.* Big belly. (FT)

wayanbara (FT)
woman's private parts.

waybala (FT, HB)
white man.
Note: From early Australian pidgin from English 'white fellow'.
• *Waybala wulan.* White man died. (HB)

waymarri (HB) ~ **waymarri** (WS)
white woman.
Note: From early Australian pidgin from English 'white Mary'.

wayngu (FT)
no good.
• *Wayngu-giya, ngalnga guyba-ya dhanhangu, gani-mundu.* They're bad, don't give them anything, they're from a long way. (FT)

widjan (RP)
empty.

wilda (CR)
cold.

windjinggara (BD)
crane.

wubidjay (FT)
young.
• *Yarala wubidjay.* Young man.

wudhagu (RP)
duck.

Wudhurraynggan (HB)
women's skin name with emu totem.

Wudhurru (HB)
men's skin name with emu totem.

wuga (CR, HS)
sleep, asleep.

wula- (CR, RP)
to die.
• *Warngu wulan.* The woman died. (HB)

wumay (RP)
good.
• *Wumay-ngan migulu.* He's a good white man. (RP)

wumay-ngunda (RP)
sweet, good.

wumbara- (GR, HB)
to sleep.
• *Wumbara-gu yani-gu.* Going for a sleep. (HB)

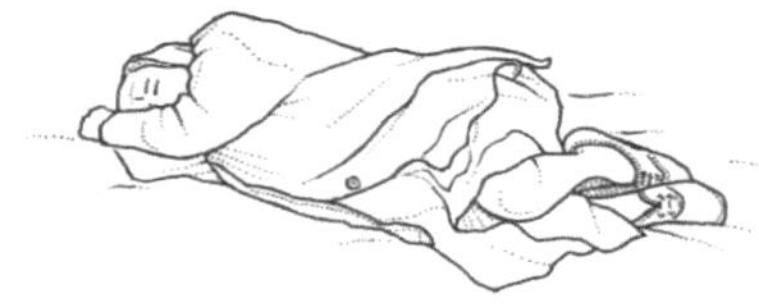

wumbararrgu (HB)
dead man.

wuna- (RP)
to lie, to lie down, to be.
• ***Gidungan wuna gamu.*** The water is too cold. (RP)

wuni- (FT)
to die.
• ***Wuni-na gaygara.*** The kangaroo died. (FT)

Wunku (HB)
men's skin name.
Note: Dove totem (HB)

Wunkuraynggan (HB)
women's skin name.
Note: Dove totem (HB)

wura (GR) ~ **waru** (BD)
kangaroo, big wallaroo.

wuriba (BD)
bee.

wurru (RP)
tree.

yabala (HB, RP)
blood.

yabu (GR, RP)
1. father. (GR)
2. mother. (RP)

yabudhana (RP)
younger sister.

yadimba- (RP)
to laugh.
• ***Bula yadimba-ya.***
Those two are laughing. (RP)

yagu (CR, HB, RP) ~ **yalnggun** (FT)
grass.

yaguy (RP)
skin.

yamani (GR, HB, RP) ~ **yamalbara** (FT)
rainbow.

yamba (CR, FT, GR, HB, RP) ~ **yambala** (FT)
camp.
• ***Yamba-wu yani-na ngaya.***
I went back to camp. (FT)

yandja- (CR)
to come.
• ***Ngani-wu gara yandja-na dhanha.*** Why did they come? (FT)
• ***Gani-mundu yandja-na yinda?*** Did you come a long way? (NEW)

yanga (CR, FT, HB)
mother.
• ***Yanga-wu garra yani-na.*** He probably went looking for his mother. (FT)

yangabara (RP)
long.
• ***Yangabara galga.*** Long spear. (RP)

yangga- (FT, HB)
to look for.
• ***Warngula-wu yangga-la ngaya.***
I'm looking for a woman. (FT)

yani- (FT, HB, HS, RP)
to go, to come.
• *Yani-na yura gunggarri?* Did you lot come from the north? (FT)

yara (FT, HB) ~ **yarala** (CR, FT)
Aboriginal man.
• *Yara yani-na gani.* The man went far away. (FT)

yarala wubidjay (FT)
young man.
• *Yarala wubidjay-ngu wangal.* The young man has a boomerang. (NEW)

yarraman (GR, RP)
horse.
Note: From early Australian pidgin.

yarraman-ngamu (GR)
horse-like.

yara (FT) ~ **yaru** (FT)
here, this.
• *Gara yara-mundu yura.* You lot are not from here. (FT)
• *Yaru-ngga nyinaya.* Sit down here. (FT)

yilbay (HS) ~ **yirrbay** (BD)
grey kangaroo.

yiliriman (RP) ~ **iliriman** (RP)
shield.

yinda- (FT)
to set (of sun).
• *Gari yinda-ya guwa.* The sun sets in the west. (FT)

yindana (RP)
for you.

yinu (RP)
your.
• *Yinu banggala.* Your spear. (NEW)

yirrbay (BD) ~ **yilbay** (HS)
grey kangaroo.

yirriyal (RP) ~ **irriyal** (RP)
tree.

yugan (HB, RP) ~ **yuganbiri** (FT)
clouds, rain.

yugila (BD, FT, HB)
star.

yungguru (HB, RP) ~ **yunggura** (BD)
kangaroo; beef.
• *Yungguru gandji-ngan.* It was stuck in the kangaroo. (RP)

yunyiman (WS)
spirit, invisible beings.
• *Galamu-galamu yani-na yambala-wu yunyiman-ngu.* Elders have gone to the spiritual home. (NEW)

yuri (FT, GR, HB, RP)
1. meat. (FT, GR, HB, RP)
2. kangaroo, game (hunted animal). (HB, FT)
• *Yuri nhaga-nyu ngali, gaygara.* We'll see this yuri, a wallaroo. (FT)

yuway (GR, RP) ~ **yuwuway** (HB)
yes.

yuwundji (RP)
ghost, spirit, devil.

11 English to Gudjal in categories

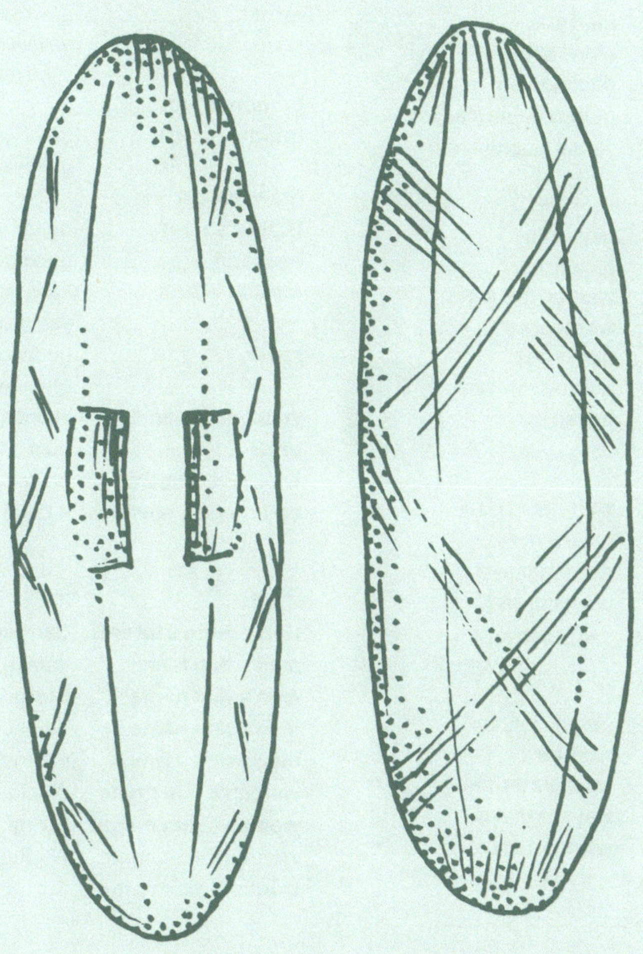

Gulmarri
'shield'

1 People

Kids and babies

baby .... ginyu (RP)
galbin (CR, FT)
child .... walbara (GR)
child, baby .... galbin (CR, FT)
children .... galbirri (FT, HB, RP)
galdjara (GR)

Men

Aboriginal man .... bama (RP)
yara (FT, HB)
yarala (CR, FT)
Aboriginal person .... mari (GR)
marri (CR, HB)
boy .... dhalmay (BD)
old man .... gulbuy bama (RP)
young man .... yarala wubidjay (FT)

Women

Aboriginal woman .... gayu (HB)
gayun (HS)
warngu (GR, RP)
warngura (FT)
girl .... banya (RP)
guguwigan (BD)
ngilan (HB)

Spirits

dead man .... wumbararrgu (HB)
male ghost .... guwi (FT)
female ghost .... guwinggan (FT)
ghost, spirit, devil .... yuwundji (RP)
spirit, invisible being .. yunyiman (WS)

White people

white man .... migulu (HB, RP)
warbun (CR)
waybala (FT, HB)
white woman .... waymarri (HB)
waymari (WS)

2 Language

our language .... Gudjal (FT, HB)
our people of Charters Towers .... Gudjalbari (GR)
to talk .... birra- (RP)
to tell .... ngubi- (FT)
noise, sound .... mungga (RP)

3 Family

aunty .... bimu (RP)
brother .... mugina (FT, RP)
cousin .... dhabu (GR)
father .... gaya (HB, HS, RP)
gayala (FT)
yabu (GR)
grandmother (mother's side) .... gami (GR)
gamiya (RP)
grandparent (father's side) .... ngadji (GR, RP)
husband .... gurrnggal (FT, HB)
mother .... yabu (RP)
yanga (CR, FT, HB)
sister .... gudhana (GR)
gudjina (GR)
younger sister .... yabudhana (RP)
uncle .... bulu (GR)
wife, sweetheart .... birrgu (BD, FT, HB, RP)
bad friends, enemies ... dabura (RP)

4 Skin names

Harry Bunn's totem .... Garrgay (HB)
men's skin name .... Wunku (HB)
men's skin name .... Gurrgila (HB)
men's skin name .... Wudhurru (HB)
men's skin name .... Gurrguru (HB)
women's skin name .... Wunkurayngga n (HB)
women's skin name .... Gurrgilaynggan (HB)
women's skin name .... Wudhurraynggan (HB)
women's skin name .... Gurrguraynggan (HB)

5 Parts of the body

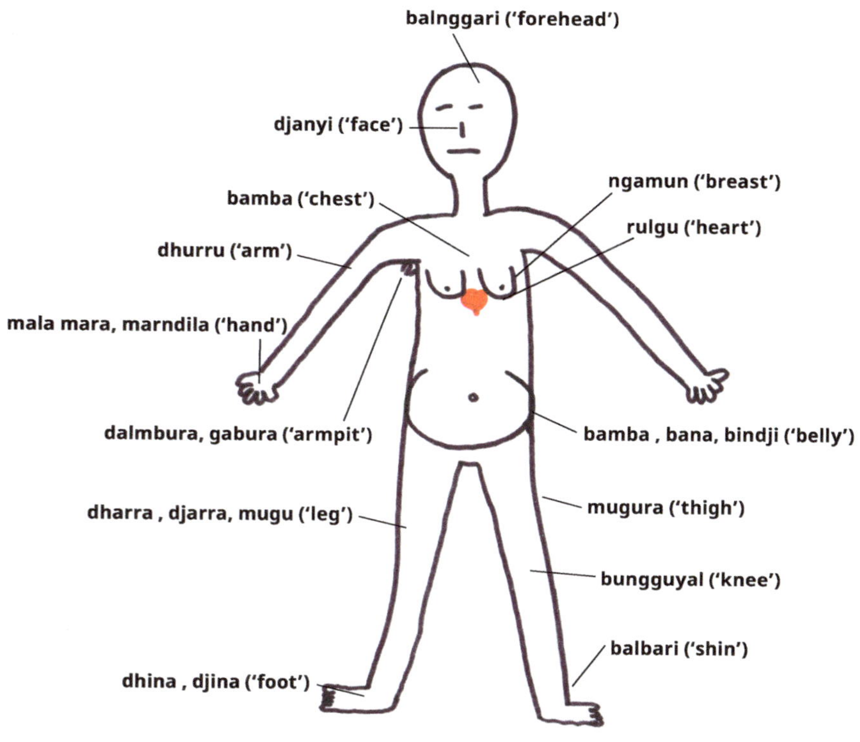

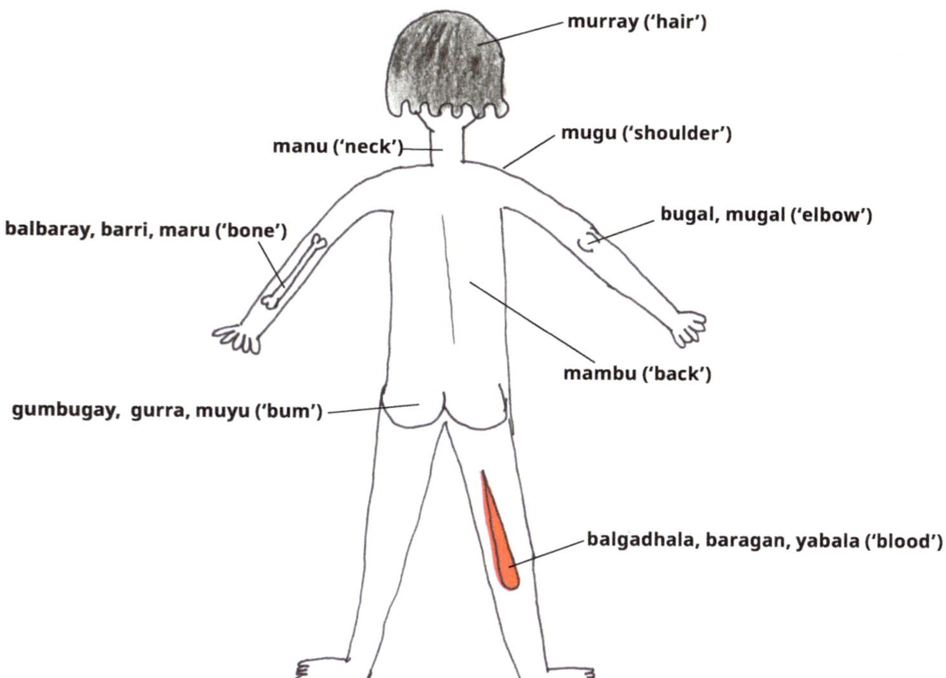

Whole body

English	Gudjal
body	bana (GR, HB, RP)
body smell	gabura (HB)

Head, face and hair

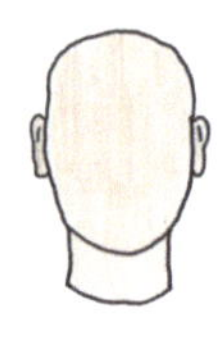
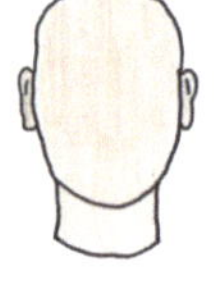

English	Gudjal
head	gada (RP)
	gadha (GR, HS)
	wanban (FT)
face	djanyi (HB)
hair	murray (HB, RP)
beard	dhalbal (RP)
	djalbara (RP)
	nganka (FT)
forehead	balnggari (HB)
	dinggal (RP)
	ngulu (RP)
ear	bina (GR)
	manga (HB)
	walu (RP)
	walumu (FT)
eye	dhili (GR)
	djili (CR, HB, RP)
eyelash	djanyin (HB)
nose	guda (RP)
	gudja (FT, HB)
mouth	dhawa (FT, RP)
	djawa (HB)
lips	nambul (CR)
teeth	dirra (GR)
	rirra (HB, RP)
tongue	birriya (RP)
	dalay (CR)
	dhalan (GR)
	dhanga(GR)
	djangin (HB)
moustache	djalbarayi (HB)

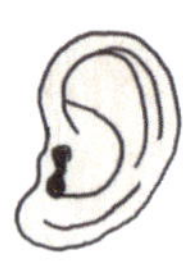

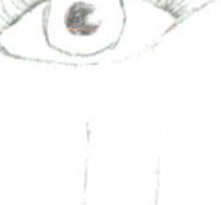

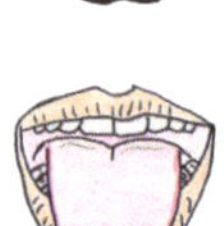
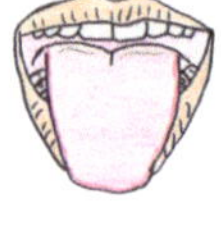
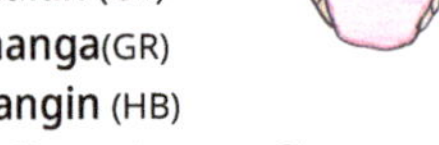

Neck and shoulders

English	Gudjal
neck	manu (FT, HB, RP)
nape, back of neck	manu ngarra (HB)
shoulder	mugu (HB)
	ngandji (RP)

Torso

English	Gudjal
back	mambu (FT, HB, RP)
belly	bamba (FT, RP)
	bana (GR, HB, RP)
	bindji (FT)
chest	bamba (FT, RP)
breasts, milk	ngamun (FT, HB, RP)

Buttocks, hips and pelvis

English	Gudjal
bottom, backside	gumbugay (HB)
	gurra (FT)
	muyu (RP)
erection	wambawuru (HB)
penis	bunga (RP)
	dhumbi (FT)
	djumbi (HB)
tail	dhumbi (FT)
	djumbi (HB)
pubic hair	djinggu (CR)
	djinggurang (FT)
testicles	galun (FT, RP)
	wadjila (RP)
woman's private parts	badhu (RP)
	budja (HB)
	djirribirri (RP)
	minga (HB, RP)
	wayanbara (FT)

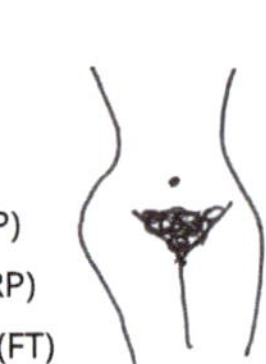

Arms and hands

English	Gudjal
arm	dhurru (FT, RP)
lower arm	barran (HB)
upper arm	djalun (HB)
armpit	dalmbura (HB)
	gabura (RP)
armpit smell	dalmbura wangga (HB)
elbow	bugal (HB)
	mugal (HB)
hand	mala (CR, GR)
	mara (HB, RP)
	marndila (FT)

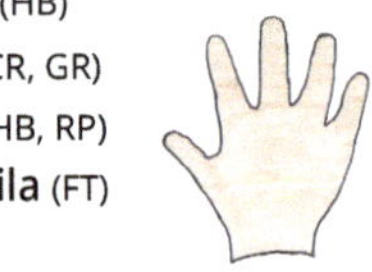

Legs and feet

English	Gudjal
leg	dharra (FT, RP)
	djarra (HB)
	mugu (RP)
thigh	mugura (FT)
knee	bungguyal (FT)
shin	balbari (FT)
foot	dhina (GR)
	djina (CR, HB, RP)

Skin and internal body parts

English	Gudjal
blood	balgadhala (FT)
	baragan (CR)
	yabala (HB, RP)
bone	balbaray (FT)
	barri (RP)
	maru (RP)

skin .... mindjan (HB)
yaguy (RP)
fat .... bunguy (RP)
dalburu (RP)
dami (CR)
dhalmira (FT)
heart .... rulgu (HB, RP)
liver .... bana (GR, HB, RP)
giba (RP)
guts .... girigira (HB)
piss, urine .... galmara (FT, HB, RP)
poo, shit .... guna (HB, RP)
guyala (FT)

6 Camp and home

camp .... yamba (CR, FT, GR, HB, RP)
yambala (FT)
corroboree .... malgarri (GR)
dancing grounds .... malbanani (RP)
fire .... buri (GR, HB)
burila (FT)
daru (CR)
gaybal (RP)
light, blaze .... milili (FT)
smoke .... dhuga (CR, RP)
dhugala (FT)
ashes .... bunba (HB, RP)

7 Food and drink

food .... mayi (GR, RP)
vegetable food, bread .... manda (GR)
mandha (FT, HB, RP)
meat .... minya (GR, HB, RP)
yuri (FT, GR, HB, RP)
kangaroo, beef .... yunggura (BD)
yungguru (HB, RP)
milk .... ngamun (GR)
water, beer .... gamu (GR)
wine .... budhulu (GR)
tobacco .... mundja (GR, RP)

8 Tools and artefacts

axe, stone tomahawk .... balgu (CR, FT, GR, HB, RP)
billycan .... gurrgarra (RP)
boomerang .... wangal (FT, GR, RP)
club .... mirru (FT)
miru (GR)
firestick .... gaybal (RP)
minggala (FT)

gun .... marrgid (RP)
knife .... gankari (FT, GR, HB, RP)
money .... badjuru (WS)
shield .... gulmarri (CR, FT)
iliriman (RP)
yiliriman (RP)
spear .... banggala (FT)
banggay (CR, FT, HB
spear (for fish) .... galga (GR, RP)
woomera .... darila (CR)
dharrila (FT)
dharrimu (FT)
stick .... dhula (GR, RP)
dhulay (RP)
yamstick, fighting stick .... dalimbirri (RP)
dhalmu (FT)

9 Clothes

belt .... gawanda (RP)
boots .... bundjurru (RP)
djinaman (RP)
clothes .... gambi (RP)
hat .... galbara (RP)
gurrigurri (FT)

10 Mammals

bandicoot .... gudjila (HB, RP)
cattle, bullock, beef .... dhumuburu (BD, GR, RP)
dingo .... ngurra (GR, HB)
wandi (GR, HB, RP)
dog .... gandu (FT, HB, HS, RP)
gandura (FT)
flying fox .... guwinggubari (BD)
horse .... yarraman (GR, RP)
kangaroo .... mangarra (RP)
wura (GR)
kangaroo rat .... bardjala (HB)
barngan (HB)
barrngala (GR, RP)
kangaroo, female grey .... gurugay (BD)
kangaroo, grey .... yilbay (HS)
yirrbay (BD)
kangaroo as meat .... yunggura (BD)
yungguru (HB, RP)
kangaroo as game (hunted animal) .... yuri (FT, HB)
pig .... gudhubaya (RP)

porcupine (echidna) .... balbirra (GR)
barrbira (FT, HB, RP)
possum .... danguru (GR)
gadharra (RP)
gadjarra (CR, FT, GR, HB)
midin (HB, RP)
sheep .... dhumba (WS)
wallaby .... badhara (GR)
rock wallaby .... bawura (BD)
bawuru (FT)
wallaroo,
old man kangaroo .... gaygara (BD, FT, HS)
gaygarra (HB, RP)
big wallaroo .... waru (BD)
wura (GR)

11 Birds

brolga .... gunumali (BD, RP)
gurralga (HB)
cockatoo .... gayambula (RP)
gayimbula (HB)
white cockatoo .... giyamara (BD, FT)
crane .... windjinggara (BD)
crow .... wadhagan (FT, RP)
wadjagan (HB)
duck .... gubiri (BD, GR, RP)
wudhagu (RP)
eaglehawk .... guridjala (BD)
emu .... gabirri (RP)
gundulu (BD, CR, FT, GR, HB, HS, RP)
hawk .... wadhubara (BD)
kookaburra .... gagubara (FT)
gugubarra (RP)
magpie .... gubura (FT)
parrot .... birrbirr (BD)
pelican .... bambabari (HB)
manbabirri (BD, RP)
plains turkey .... dharguy (RP)
djarrguyn (HB)
scrub turkey .... girruwan (HB)
sparrowhawk .... garrgay (HB)
willy wagtail .... djigankara (FT)
egg .... bambu (RP)
gugudji (HB)
wanmalga (FT)
emu egg .... wanmalga gundulu (FT)

12 Reptiles and frogs

blue-tongue lizard .... banggarra (GR, RP)
frilled lizard .... bindjiri (FT)
brown lizard with rough skin .... ngandharri (FT)
small lizard on tree .... galmanda (HB)
spotted bull goanna .... dhagan (GR, HB)
djagan (HB)
sand goanna .... dhagay (BD, FT, HB, RP)
djagay (HB)
snake (any) .... dambal (RP)
munda (GR)
snake, carpet snake .... gabu (FT, HB)
gabul (BD, FT)
tree snake .... gurrgalbara (BD)
turtle .... banggurru (BD, HB, RP)
frog .... ganal (HB)
wagwuy (RP)

13 Fish

black bream .... baylbira (BD)
catfish .... gunggala (BD)
eel .... wagal (BD, HB, RP)
fish .... guyu (FT, GR, HB, HS, RP)
guyun (BD)
perch .... gurrbara (BD)

14 Insects and small creatures

bee .... gugara (BD)
wuriba (BD)
quiet bee .... wadhabara (BD)
lice .... marrbu (HB, RP)
mugagan (HB)
grasshopper, locust .... nyiri-nyiri (HB, RP)
mosquito .... gigabidi (CR)
small flying insect .... ngandarri (RP)
tree grub .... djambu (RP)
wasp .... dhamarra (RP)

15 Plants

bora tree .... bura (FT)
fig tree .... baygari (FT)
ironbark tree .... galgan (FT)
plum tree .... bundjibara (FT)

stick .... **dhula** (GR, RP)
dhulay (RP)
tree .... **dhula** (GR, RP)
dhulay (RP)
irriyal (RP)
wurru (RP)

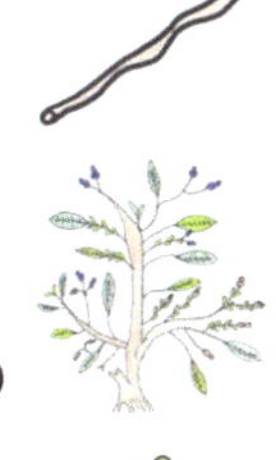

grass .... **yagu** (CR, HB, RP)
yalnggun (FT)
burnt grass .... **madhira** (BD)

16 Country

dust, sand .... **bunba** (HB, RP)
ground .... **nhani** (RP)
nhanira (FT)
hole .... **bimbala** (FT)
mountain .... **bubuyal** (FT)
big mountains .... **bubudhala** (FT)
name of mountain at Charters Towers .... **Mural** (FT)
paint used for corroboree .... **maga** (RP)
river .... **birula** (FT)
salt water .... **gudjarra** (FT)
sand .... **galbadhura** (FT)
scrub .... **mudhara** (FT)
stone .... **bari** (CR, FT, HS)
barri (HB, RP)
water .... **bana** (GR)
gabari (FT)
galmun (FT)
gamu (CR, FT, GR, HS, RP)
ngalu (RP)

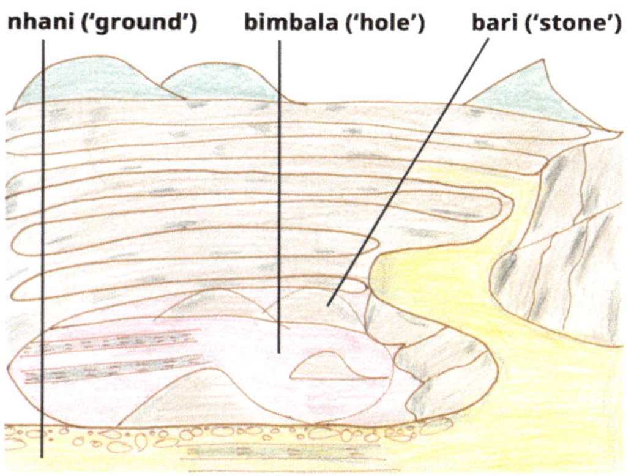

17 Sky and weather

sun .... **gari** (FT, HS)
garri (HB, RP)
gayala (BD, CR)
moon .... **balalbara** (BD, FT)
balanu (CR, HB, HS, RP)
star .... **djamban** (RP)
yugila (BD, FT, HB)
rainbow .... **yamani** (GR, HB, RP)
yamalbara (FT)
clouds .... **yugan** (HB, RP)
yuganbiri (FT)
rain .... **bana** (GR)
gabari (FT)
yugan (HB, RP)
yuganbiri (FT)
lightning .... **madjala** (FT)
thunder .... **nyinggala** (FT)
rambu (RP)
weather .... **bandara** (RP)
wind .... **gawaray** (FT)
guru (GR)
mimirri (CR)

18 Time and season

morning .... **garingga** (HB, RP)
sunset, gone dark .... **gunkay** (HB)
dark .... **gunda** (HB, HS, RP)
tomorrow .... **garralay** (FT)
wintertime .... **budhula** (GR)

19 Direction

above, up .... **ngarra** (RP)
close, alongside .... **birri** (HB)
far .... **gani** (FT)
here .... **yara** (FT)
yaru (FT)
there, that .... **nguna** (FT)
this, that .... **marangan** (RP)

20 Compass directions

north .... **gunggarri** (FT, RP)
south .... **gulbila** (FT, HB)
east .... **wanggarri** (HB)
west .... **guwa** (FT)

21 Numbers and counting

1, one .... nyungkaru (HS)
nyunkul (HB, RP)
2, two .... bulari (HB, HS, RP)
2, two; or 3, three .... gudjarra (HB)
3, three .... gudbara (FT, HS)
4, four; or several .... marrgabala (FT)
muga (HS)
big mob, very many .... guyba-guyba (FT)
plenty .... ngunmari (RP)

22 Yes and no

maybe .... garra (FT)
no .... manda (FT)
no, don't .... gara (GR, HB)
garra (RP)
not, don't .... ngalnga (RP)
yes .... yuway (GR, RP)
yuwuway (HB)

23 Questions

what kind? .... ngani-mbara (FT)
what? .... ngana (RP)
ngani (RP)
where? .... wandha (FT, RP)
where at? .... wandha-rru (RP)
where from? .... wandha-mundu (FT)
who? .... ngani (RP)
wanyu (FT)
whose? .... wanyu-ngunda (FT)
why? what for? .... ngani-wu (FT)
why? wherefore? .... wandha-rri (RP)

24 Properties

Size and speed

big .... warul (FT)
warulgaram (FT)
long .... gulgandjarra (FT)
yangabara (RP)
small, little .... ganggura (CR)
fast, quick .... wabagara (BD)
quick, quickly .... ngurri (FT)

Colour

dark .... gunda (HB, HS, RP)
white .... gurrgu (RP)
grey .... baringgalay (FT)

Temperature and texture

cold .... gidu (RP)
wilda (CR)
dirty .... nanimbarra (RP)
empty .... widjan (RP)
full .... badji (RP)
rough .... walmay (BD)
walwa (HB, RP)
sharp .... birrgalbay (FT)

Value

good .... dharibara (FT)
waminbiri (BD)
wumay (RP)
bad, no good .... gadja (GR)
garrangandu (RP)
walmay (BD)
walwa (HB, RP)
wayngu (FT)

Human qualities

anger, bad temper .... guli (FT, RP)
cheeky .... ngayngarra (FT)
deaf .... binagari (WS)
happy .... gunarri (RP)
horse-like .... yarraman-ngamu (GR)
love .... gawarri (RP)
sleep, asleep .... wuga (CR, HS)
old (person) .... galamu (FT)

Food qualities

bitter, no good .... garrangandu (RP)
sweet, good .... wumay-ngunda (RP)
raw .... gunka (HB, RP)
cooked .... waduwingan (RP)
greedy, hungry .... wandjabirri (RP)

25 Verbs

Verbs of talking and singing

to talk .... birra- (RP)
to tell .... ngubi- (FT)
to laugh .... yadimba- (RP)
to shout .... gawa- (RP)
to sing .... bayari- (RP)

Verbs of movement

to come .... wanba- (FT)
yandja- (CR)
to go .... yani- (FT, HB, HS, RP)
to go away,
to go far .... ganibi- (RP)
to jump .... dhulba- (RP)
to dance .... namba- (RP)
to play .... gayinmadhara- (FT)
to fall .... dhanda- (FT)
to rise (of sun) .... waga- (FT)
to set (of sun) .... yinda- (FT)

Verbs of doing to

to bite .... badha- (FT)
to eat .... bida- (RP)
to break .... gundji- (RP)
gunma- (RP)
to carry, to take .... gandji- (FT)
to cut .... ngura- (FT)
to hit, to kill .... balga- (RP)
guni- (FT)
to get, to make,
to light .... muga- (RP)
to make .... miranga- (FT)
to give, to put .... guyba- (HB)
to push .... bubudha- (FT)
to shake .... bubudhali- (FT)
dhandhari- (FT)
to let go .... bindamba- (FT)

Verbs of rest and staying

to stay .... dhana- (FT)
to sit down, to stay .... nyina- (HB, RP)
to stand .... djana- (HB)
to tire, to get tired .... bigali- (HB)
to sleep .... bundji- (RP)
wumbara- (GR, HB)
to lie, to lie down,
to be .... wuna- (RP)
to die .... wula- (CR, RP)
wuni- (FT)

Verbs of feeling

to ache .... djidji- (RP)
to anger,
to get angry .... gulibi- (RP)
to cry .... ngiduwi- (HB)

Verbs of perception

to hear .... ngambi- (FT)
to listen .... mungga- (RP)
to see, to look .... nhaga- (HB, RP)
to look at,
to stare at .... djundjula- (RP)
to look for .... yangga- (FT, HB)

12 English to Gudjal finder list

In this finder list, the Gudjal words listed after each English word all share the same or similar meanings. Words separated by commas are different pronunciations of the same word. Words separated by a semicolon (;) are different words that have either the same or a similar meaning. When a Gudjal word is found with the finder list, its full entry should then be consulted in the main Gudjal to English dictionary.

Gurrigurri
'hat'

Aa

Aboriginal
- man ... bama (RP); yara (FT, HB), yarala (CR, FT)
- person ... mari (GR), marri (CR, HB)
- woman ... gayu (HB), gayun (HS); warngu (GR, RP), warngura (FT)

above, up ... ngarra (RP)
ache, be in pain ... djidji- (RP)
alongside, close ... birri (HB)
anger, bad temper ... guli (FT, RP)
angry, get angry ... gulibi- (RP)
arm ... dhurru (FT, RP)
- lower arm ... barran (HB)
- upper arm ... djalun (HB)

armpit ... dalmbura (HB); gabura (RP)
- armpit smell ... dalmbura wangga (HB)

ashes ... bunba (HB, RP)
aunty ... bimu (RP)
away
- go away, go far ... ganibi- (RP)

axe
- stone tomahawk, axe .. balgu (CR, FT, GR, HB, RP)

Bb

baby ... galbin (CR, FT); ginyu (RP)
back, backbone ... mambu (FT, HB, RP)
backside, bottom ... gumbugay (HB); gurra (FT); muyu (RP)
bad
- no good ... gadja (GR); wayngu (FT)
- no good, bad, rough ... walmay (BD), walwa (HB, RP)
- no good, bitter ... garrangandu (RP)
- bad friends, enemies .. dabura (RP)
- bad temper, anger ... guli (FT, RP)

bandicoot ... gudjila (HB, RP)
be, lie down ... wuna- (RP)
beard ... dhalbal (RP), djalbara (RP); nganka (FT)
bee ... gugara (BD); wuriba (BD)
- quiet bee ... wadhabara (BD)

beef
- beef, kangaroo ... yunggura (BD),
- ... yungguru (HB, RP)
- beef, cattle, bullock ... dhumuburu (BD, GR, RP)

beer ... gamu (GR)
belly ... bamba (FT, RP); bana (GR, HB, RP); bindji (FT)
belt ... gawanda (RP)
big ... warul (FT), warulgaram (FT)
big mob, many ... guyba-guyba (FT)
billycan ... gurrgarra (RP)
bite ... badha- (FT)
bitter ... garrangandu (RP)
blaze, light ... milili (FT)
blood ... balgadhala (FT); baragan (CR); yabala (HB, RP)
blue-tongue lizard ... banggarra (GR, RP)
body
- body ... bana (GR, HB, RP)
- body smell ... gabura (HB)

bone ... balbaray (FT); barri (RP); maru (RP)
boomerang ... wangal (FT, GR, RP)
boots ... bundjurru (RP); djinaman (RP)
bora tree ... bura (FT)
bottom, backside ... gumbugay (HB); gurra (FT); muyu (RP)
boy ... dhalmay (BD)
bread ... manda (GR), mandha (FT, HB, RP)
break ... gundji- (RP); gunma- (RP)
breasts ... ngamun (FT, HB, RP)
brolga ... gunumali (BD, RP); gurralga (HB)
brother ... mugina (FT, RP)
bullock, beef, cattle ... dhumuburu (BD, GR, RP)
bum ... gumbugay (HB); gurra (FT); muyu (RP)
burnt grass ... madhira (BD)
bush, scrub ... mudhara (FT)

Cc

camp, a camp ... yamba (CR, FT, GR, HB, RP), yambala (FT)
carpet snake ... gabu (FT, HB), gabul (BD, FT)
carry ... gandji- (FT)
catfish ... gunggala (BD)
cattle, bullock, beef ... dhumuburu (BD, GR, RP)
Charters Towers ... Mural (FT)
cheeky ... ngayngarra (FT)
chest ... bamba (FT, RP)
child ... galbin (CR, FT); walbara (GR)
- children ... galbirri (FT, HB, RP); galdjara (GR)

close, alongside ... birri (HB)
clothes ... gambi (RP)
clouds ... yugan (HB, RP), yuganbiri (FT)
club ... mirru (FT), miru (GR)
cockatoo ... gayambula (RP), gayimbula (HB)

white cockatoo .... giyamara (BD, FT)
cold .... gidu (RP); wilda (CR)
come .... wanba- (FT); yandja- (CR)
cooked .... waduwingan (RP)
corroboree .... malgarri (GR)
cousin .... dhabu (GR)
cow, bullock, beef .... dhumuburu (BD, GR, RP)
crane .... windjinggara (BD)
crow .... wadhagan (FT, RP), wadjagan (HB)
cry .... ngiduwi- (HB)
cut .... ngura- (FT)

Dd

dad .... gaya (HB, HS, RP), gayala (FT); yabu (GR)
dance
to dance .... namba- (RP)
dancing grounds .... malbanani (RP)
dark .... gunda (HB, HS, RP)
sunset, gone dark .... gunkay (HB)
dead man .... wumbararrgu (HB)
deaf .... binagari (WS)
devil .... yuwundji (RP)
die .... wula- (CR, RP); wuni- (FT)
dingo .... ngurra (GR, HB); wandi (GR, HB, RP)
dirty .... nanimbarra (RP)
dog .... gandu (FT, HB, HS, RP), gandura (FT)
don't
don't, no .... gara (GR, HB), garra (RP)
don't, not .... ngalnga (RP)
duck, a duck .... gubiri (BD, GR, RP); wudhagu (RP)
dust .... bunba (HB, RP)

Ee

eaglehawk .... guridjala (BD)
ear .... bina (GR); manga (HB); walu (RP), walumu (FT)
east .... wanggarri (HB)
eat .... bida- (RP)
eel .... wagal (BD, HB, RP)
egg .... bambu (RP); gugudji (HB); wanmalga (FT)
emu egg .... wanmalga gundulu (FT)
elbow .... bugal (HB), mugal (HB)
empty .... widjan (RP)
emu .... gabirri (RP); gundulu (BD, CR, FT, GR, HB, HS, RP)
emu egg .... wanmalga gundulu (FT)
enemies, bad friends .... dabura (RP)
erection .... wambawuru (HB)
eye .... dhili (GR), djili (CR, HB, RP)
eyelash .... djanyin (HB)

Ff

face .... djanyi (HB)
fall .... dhanda- (FT)
far
far away .... gani (FT)
go away, go far .... ganibi- (RP)
fast, quick .... wabagara (BD)
fat .... bunguy (RP); dalburu (RP); dami (CR), dhalmira (FT)
father .... gaya (HB, HS, RP), gayala (FT); yabu (GR)
female
Aboriginal woman .... gayu (HB), gayun (HS); warngu (GR, RP), warngura (FT)
white woman .... waymarri (HB)
female ghost .... guwinggan (FT)
female grey kangaroo .... gurugay (BD)
fig tree .... baygari (FT)
fighting stick .... dhalmu (FT)
fire
fire .... buri (GR, HB), burila (FT); daru (CR)
fire, firestick .... gaybal (RP)
firestick .... gaybal (RP); minggala (FT)
fish .... guyu (FT, GR, HB, HS, RP), guyun (BD)
black bream .... baylbira (BD)
catfish .... gunggala (BD)
flying fox .... guwinggubari (BD)
food .... mayi (GR, RP)
foot .... dhina (GR), djina (CR, HB, RP)
for .... -wu, -gu
for me .... ngaygunda (RP)
for you .... yindana (RP)
for them .... dhanangu (FT)
forehead .... balnggari (HB); dinggal (RP); ngulu (RP)
four, or several .... marrgabala (FT); muga (HS)
frilled lizard .... bindjiri (FT)
frog .... ganal (HB); wagwuy (RP)

full..........badji (RP)

Gg

game
kangaroo, game (hunted animal)..........yuri (HB, FT)
get, make..........muga- (RP)
ghost, spirit..........yuwundji (RP), yunyiman (WS)
female ghost..........guwinggan (FT)
male ghost..........guwi (FT)
girl..........banya (RP); guguwigan (BD); ngilan (HB)
give..........guyba- (HB)
go..........yani- (FT, HB, HS, RP)
go away, go far..........ganibi- (RP)
goanna
spotted one..........dhagan (GR, HB), djagan (HB)
sand goanna..........dhagay (BD, FT, HB, RP), djagay (HB)
good..........dharibara (FT); waminbiri (BD); wumay (RP)
good, sweet..........wumay-ngunda (RP)
grandmother
mother's mother..........gami (GR), gamiya (RP)
father's parent..........ngadji (GR, RP)
grandfather
father's parent..........ngadji (GR, RP)
grass..........yagu (CR, HB, RP), yalnggun (FT)
burnt grass..........madhira (BD)
grasshopper..........nyiri-nyiri (HB, RP)
greedy..........wandjabirri (RP)
grey..........baringgalay (FT)
grey kangaroo, female..........gurugay (BD)
ground..........nhani (RP), nhanira (FT)
grub
tree grub..........djambu (RP)
gun..........marrgid (RP)
guts..........girigira (HB)

Hh

hair..........murray (HB, RP)
pubic hair..........djinggu (CR), djinggurang (FT)
hand..........mala (CR, GR), mara (HB, RP); marndila (FT)
happy..........gunarri (RP)
hat..........galbara (RP); gurrigurri (FT)
hawk..........wadhubara (BD)
eaglehawk..........guridjala (BD)
sparrowhawk..........garrgay (HB)
head..........gada (RP), gadha (GR, HS); wanban (FT)
hear..........ngambi- (FT)
heart..........rulgu (HB, RP)
here..........yara (FT), yaru (FT)
hit..........balga- (RP)
hole..........bimbala (FT)
horse..........yarraman (GR, RP)
horse-like..........yarraman-ngamu (GR)
hungry..........wandjabirri (RP)
husband..........gurrnggal (FT, HB)

Ii

I..........ngaya (FT, HB)
insect..........ngandarri (RP)
ironbark tree..........galgan (FT)

Jj

jump..........dhulba- (RP)

Kk

kangaroo..........mangarra (RP); wura (GR)
kangaroo meat, beef...yunggura (BD), yungguru (HB, RP)
kangaroo, game (hunted animal)..........yuri (HB, FT)
grey kangaroo..........yilbay (HS), yirrbay (BD)
grey kangaroo, female..........gurugay (BD)
kangaroo rat..........bardjala (HB); barngan (HB); barrngala (GR, RP)
kill..........balga- (RP); guni- (FT)
knee..........bungguyal (FT)
knife..........gankari (FT, GR, HB, RP)
kookaburra..........gagubara (FT), gugubarra (RP)

Ll

laugh, to laugh..........yadimba- (RP)
leg..........dharra (FT, RP), djarra (HB); mugu (RP)

let go .... bindamba- (FT)
lice .... marrbu (HB, RP); mugagan (HB)
lie, lie down, be .... wuna- (RP)
light (a fire) .... muga- (RP)
light, blaze .... milili (FT)
lightning .... madjala (FT)
lips .... nambul (CR)
listen .... mungga- (RP)
little .... ganggura (CR)
liver .... bana (GR, HB, RP); giba (RP)
lizard
  blue-tongue lizard .... banggarra (GR, RP)
  brown lizard with rough skin .... ngandharri (FT)
  frilled lizard .... bindjiri (FT)
  small lizard on tree .... galmanda (HB)
locust .... nyiri-nyiri (HB, RP)
long .... gulgandjarra (FT); yangabara (RP)
look
  see, look .... nhaga- (HB, RP)
  look at .... djundju- (RP)
  look for .... yangga- (FT, HB)
lots .... guyba-guyba (FT)
love .... gawarri (RP)

Mm

magpie .... gubura (FT)
make
  make .... miranga- (FT)
  make, get, light .... muga- (RP)
male ghost .... guwi (FT)
man
  Aboriginal man .... bama (RP); yara (FT, HB), yarala (CR, FT)
  dead man .... wumbararrgu (HB)
  men .... ganya (HB)
  old man .... gulbuy bama (RP)
  white man .... migulu (HB, RP); warbun (CR); waybala (FT, HB)
  young man .... yarala wubidjay (FT)
many, big mob .... guyba-guyba (FT)
maybe .... garra (FT)
me
  I .... ngaya (FT, HB)
  me .... nganya (HB)
  for me, to me, myself .... ngaygunda (RP)
meat .... minya (GR, HB, RP)
  meat, game .... yuri (FT, GR, HB, RP)
milk .... ngamun (GR)
money .... badjuru (WS)
moon .... balalbara (BD, FT); balanu (CR, HB, HS, RP)
morning .... garingga (HB, RP)
mosquito .... gigabidi (CR)
mother .... yabu (RP); yanga (CR, FT, HB)
mountain .... bubuyal (FT)
  big mountains .... bubudhala (FT)
moustache .... djalbarayi (HB)
mouth .... dhawa (FT, RP), djawa (HB)
mum .... yabu (RP); yanga (CR, FT, HB)
myself .... ngaygunda (RP)

Nn

nan
  mother's mother .... gami (GR), gamiya (RP)
  father's parent .... ngadji (GR, RP)
nape, back of neck .... manu ngarra (HB)
neck .... manu (FT, HB, RP)
  back of neck .... manu ngarra (HB)
no .... manda (FT)
  no, don't .... gara (GR, HB), garra (RP)
  not, don't .... ngalnga (RP)
noise .... mungga (RP)
north .... gunggarri (FT, RP)
nose .... guda (RP), gudja (FT, HB)

Oo

old
  old (person) .... galamu (FT)
  old man .... gulbuy bama (RP)
  old man kangaroo .... gaygara (BD, FT, HS), gaygarra (HB, RP)
one .... nyunkul (HB, RP), nyungkaru (HS)

Pp

pain, aching .... djidji- (RP)
paint used for corroboree .... maga (RP)
parrot .... birrbirr (BD)
pelican .... bambabari (HB); manbabirri (BD, RP)

penis..........bunga (RP); dhumbi (FT), djumbi (HB)
perch..........gurrbara (BD)
person
Aboriginal..........mari (GR), marri (CR, HB)
pig..........gudhubaya (RP)
piss, urine..........galmara (FT, HB, RP)
plains turkey..........dharguy (RP); djarrguyn (HB)
play, to play..........gayinmadhara- (FT)
plenty..........ngunmari (RP)
plum tree..........bundjibara (FT)
poo..........guna (HB, RP); guyala (FT)
porcupine (echidna)..........barrbira (FT, HB, RP); balbirra (GR)
possum..........danguru (GR); gadharra (RP), gadjarra (CR, FT, GR, HB); midin (HB, RP)
private parts
— woman's..........badhu (RP); budja (HB); djirribirri (RP); minga (HB, RP); wayanbara (FT)
private parts — man's
penis..........bunga (RP); dhumbi (FT), djumbi (HB)
testicles..........galun (FT, RP)
probably..........garra (FT)
pubic hair..........djinggu (CR), djinggurang (FT)
push..........bubudha- (FT)
put, to put..........guyba- (HB)

Qq

quick, quickly..........wabagara (BD); ngurri (FT)
quiet bee..........wadhabara (BD)

Rr

rain
water..........bana (GR); gabari (FT)
clouds..........yugan (HB, RP), yuganbiri (FT)
rainbow..........yamalbara (FT), yamani (GR, HB, RP)
raw..........gunka (HB, RP)
rise (of sun)..........waga- (FT)
river..........birula (FT)
rock..........bari (CR, FT, HS), barri (HB, RP)
rock wallaby..........bawura (BD), bawuru (FT)
rough, no good..........walmay (BD), walwa (HB, RP)

Ss

salt water..........gudjarra (FT)
sand..........bunba (HB, RP); galbadhura (FT)
sand goanna..........dhagay (BD, FT, HB, RP), djagay (HB)
scrub, bush..........mudhara (FT)
scrub turkey..........girruwan (HB)
see..........nhaga- (HB, RP)
set (of sun)..........yinda- (FT)
shake..........bubudhali- (FT); dhandhari- (FT)
sharp..........birrgalbay (FT)
sheep..........dhumba (WS)
shield..........gulmarri (CR, FT); yiliriman (RP), iliriman (RP)
shin..........balbari (FT)
shit..........guna (HB, RP); guyala (FT)
shoulder..........mugu (HB); ngandji (RP)
shout, to shout..........gawa- (RP)
sing, to sing..........bayari- (RP)
sister..........gudhana (GR), gudjina (GR)
younger sister..........yabudhana (RP)
sit down..........nyina- (HB, RP)
skin, body skin..........mindjan (HB); yaguy (RP)
sleep, to sleep..........bundji- (RP); wumbara- (GR, HB)
asleep..........wuga (CR, HS)
small..........ganggura (CR)
smell
of the armpit..........dalmbura wangga (HB)
of the body..........gabura (HB)
smoke..........dhuga (CR, RP), dhugala (FT)
snake (any)..........dambal (RP); gabu (FT, HB), gabul (BD, FT); munda (GR)
carpet snake..........gabu (FT, HB), gabul (BD, FT)
tree snake..........gurrgalbara (BD)
south..........gulbila (FT, HB)
sparrowhawk..........garrgay (HB)
spear, a spear..........banggala (FT), banggay (CR, FT, HB)
spear (for fish)..........galga (GR, RP)
spirit, ghost..........yuwundji (RP), yunyiman (WS)
stand, to stand..........djana- (HB)
star..........djamban (RP); yugila (BD, FT, HB)
stare at..........djundjula- (RP)
stay..........dhana- (FT)
sit down, stay..........nyina- (HB, RP)
stick
tree, stick..........dhula (GR, RP), dhulay (RP)
fighting stick..........dhalmu (FT)
yam stick,
digging stick..........dalimbirri (RP)

stone .... bari (CR, FT, HS), barri (HB, RP)
sun .... gari (FT, HS), garri (HB, RP); gayala (BD, CR)
sundown .... gunkay (HB)
sunset .... gunkay (HB)
sweet, good .... wumay-ngunda (RP)
sweetheart, wife .... birrgu (BD, FT, HB, RP)

Tt

tail .... dhumbi (FT), djumbi (HB)
take, to take .... gandji- (FT)
talk, to talk .... birra- (RP)
teeth .... dirra (GR), rirra (HB, RP)
tell .... ngubi- (FT)
testicles .... galun (FT, RP)
that
  this, that .... marangan (RP)
  there, that .... nguna, nguni (FT)
there, that .... nguna, nguni (FT)
they
  those two .... bula (RP)
  they all .... dhanha (FT)
thigh .... mugura (FT)
this
  this, that .... marangan (RP)
  here, this .... yara, yaru (FT)
three .... gurrbara (FT, HS)
throat .... manu (FT, HB, RP)
thunder .... nyinggala (FT); rambu (RP)
tired, become tired .... bigali- (HB)
to me .... ngaygunda (RP)
tobacco .... mundja (GR, RP)
tomahawk
  stone tomahawk, axe .... balgu (CR, FT, GR, HB, RP)
tomorrow .... garralay (FT)
tongue .... birriya (RP); dalay (CR), dhalan (GR); dhanga (GR), djangin (HB)
torso .... bamba (FT, RP)
tree .... irriyal (RP), yirriyal (RP); wurru (RP); dhula (GR, RP), dhulay (RP)
  tree grub .... djambu (RP)
  tree snake .... gurrgalbara (BD)
turkey
  plains turkey .... dharguy (RP), djarrguyn (HB)
  scrub turkey .... girruwan (HB)
turtle .... banggurru (BD, HB, RP)
twilight .... gunkay (HB)
two .... bulari (HB, HS, RP)
  two or three .... gudjarra (HB)

Uu

uncle .... bulu (GR)
up, above .... ngarra (RP)
urine, piss .... galmara (FT, HB, RP)

Vv

vegetable food .... manda (GR), mandha (FT, HB, RP)

Ww

wallaby (any) .... badhara (GR)
  rock wallaby .... bawura (BD), bawuru (FT)
wallaroo
  big wallaroo .... waru (BD), wura (GR)
  old male wallaroo .... gaygara (BD, FT, HS), gaygarra (HB, RP)
wasp .... dhamarra (RP)
water .... bana (GR); gabari (FT); galmun (FT); gamu (CR, FT, GR, HS, RP); ngalu (RP)
  rain .... bana (GR); gabari (FT); yugan (HB, RP), yuganbiri (FT)
  salt water .... gudjarra (FT)
we
  we two .... ngali (FT)
  we all .... nganha (FT)
weather .... bandara (RP)
west .... guwa (FT)
what? .... ngana (RP)
  what? who? .... ngani (RP)
  what for? why? .... ngani-wu (FT)
  what kind? .... ngani-mbara (FT)
where? .... wandha (FT, RP), wandja (HB)
  where at? .... wandha-rru (RP)
  where from? .... wandha-mundu (FT)
white
  colour white .... gurrgu (RP)
  white cockatoo .... giyamara (BD, FT)
  white man .... migulu (HB, RP); warbun (CR); waybala (FT, HB)
  white woman .... waymarri (HB), waymari (WS)
who? .... wanhu, wanyu (FT)
  who? what? .... ngani (RP)
  whose? .... wanyu-ngunda (FT)
why? what for? .... ngani-wu (FT)

why? wherefore? .... wandha-rri (RP)
wife
wife, sweetheart.......... birrgu (BD, FT, HB, RP)
wild
anger, bad temper ...... guli (FT, RP)
angry, get angry.......... gulibi- (RP)
willy wagtail................ djigankara (FT)
wind.............................. mimirri (CR); gawaray (FT); guru (GR)
wine.............................. budhulu (GR)
wintertime................... budhula (GR)
woman
Aboriginal woman....... gayu (HB), gayun (HS); warngu (GR, RP), warngura (FT)
white woman............... waymarri (HB)
woman's private parts .... badhu (RP); budja (HB); djirribirri (RP); minga (HB, RP); wayanbara (FT)
woomera...................... darila (CR), dharrila (FT); dharrimu (FT)

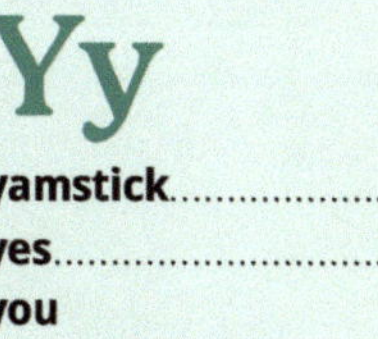

yamstick........................ dalimbirri (RP)
yes................................. yuway (GR, RP), yuwuway (HB)
you
you (singular) .... yinda (FT)
you two........................ yubala (FT)
you lot.......................... yura (FT)
for you .... yindana (RP)
young man.................... yarala wubidjay (FT)
younger sister............. yabudhana (RP)

Further reading and listening

Reading

Babidge, S, P Dallachy & V Alberts 2007, *Written true, not gammon! A history of Aboriginal Charters Towers*, Black Ink Press, Thuringowa, Queensland.

Kell, J & S Gagau 2022 (19 October) 'Buried in the sand: digging deep into Gudjal language and culture', podcast, https://anchor.fm/toksave-culture-talks/episodes/Buried-in-the-Sand-Digging-deep-into-Gudjal-language-and-culture-e1pffup/a-a8nbff3

Lukin, G 1886, 'No 122: Clarke River', in EM Curr 1886–87, *The Australian race*, Volume 2, pp 436–37, John Ferres.

Meston, A c.1900, Homestead blacks, Hughenden line, unpublished manuscript, State Library of Queensland.

Santo, WC 2006a, *Gudjal book of birds*, Black Ink Press, Thuringowa, Queensland.

Santo, WC 2006b, *My country: in Gudjal and English*, Black Ink Press, Thuringowa, Queensland.

Santo, WC 2006c, *Gudjal book of animals,* Black Ink Press, Thuringowa, Queensland.

Santo, WC 2006d, *Gudjal language pocket dictionary*, Black Ink Press, Thuringowa, Queensland.

Santo, WC 2016, *Maggie and Charley Santo: the history of the Santo Family of Charters Towers*, Keeaira Press, Southport, Queensland.

Stockley, T 2006, Body parts and their names (Gudjal); Gudjal sounds: get them right; Kinship and family: Gugu-Badhun and Gudjal; Personal and possessive pronouns: practice sentences, Questions and answers using pronouns, unpublished manuscript, North Queensland Regional Aboriginal Corporation Language Centre, Cairns, Queensland. A copy is held at the Australian Institute for Aboriginal and Torres Strait Islander Studies, Canberra, within the call number: MS 4820.

Sutton, P 1970, Transcription of Field Tapes No. 70/33–36, AIATSIS tape nos. SUTTON_P01-001911–001913, unpublished manuscripts held at the Australian Institute for Aboriginal and Torres Strait Islander Studies, Canberra.

Sutton, P 1973, Gugu-Badhun and its neighbours: a linguistic salvage study, Master's thesis, Macquarie University, Sydney. Australian Institute for Aboriginal and Torres Strait Islander Studies, Canberra, call number: MS 694.

Tsunoda, T 2012, *A grammar of Warrongo*, Mouton Grammar Library Volume 53, De Gruyter Mouton, Berlin, https://doi.org/10.1515/9783110238778

Tsunoda, T 1974, Fieldwork report [to AIAS], unpublished manuscript held at the Australian Institute for Aboriginal and Torres Strait Islander Studies, Canberra, call number: MS 709.

Tsunoda, T nd, Language materials from Queensland, Western Australia, and Northern Territory, 1971–2006, unpublished manuscript held at the Australian Institute for Aboriginal and Torres Strait Islander Studies, Canberra, call number: MS 5021.

Tsunoda, T 1983, Verbal inflectional morphology in historical linguistics: a case study in the Upper Herbert—Burdekin languages of north Queensland, unpublished manuscript held at the Australian Institute for Aboriginal and Torres Strait Islander Studies, Canberra, call number: PMS 3820.

White, EED c. 1919, Aboriginal names N. Kennedy, Q., from a notebook of EED White of Bluff Downs dated sometime just before 1920.

Listening

Santo, WC, A Anderson, M Turpin 2021, Fifty Words Project Gudjal words, https://50words.online. Research Unit for Indigenous Language, University of Melbourne.

Santo, W, A Anderson, M Turpin 2021 (17 February), *Relearning Gudjal through archival materials*, video presentation, PARADISEC@100, Sydney, https://www.youtube.com/watch?v=4RRbl0A-D6M

Archival Audio Materials

List of Gudjal audio held at the Australian Institute for Aboriginal and Torres Strait Islander Studies, Canberra. All these have been transcribed by Alex Anderson and deposited in AIATSIS.

Speaker	Date	Place	Duration	AIATSIS Accession no.
Freddie Toomba	1970	Palm Island	57m 30s	SUTTON_P01-001913A
Freddie Toomba	1970	Palm Island	31m	SUTTON_P01-001913B
Ranji Pope	1970	Charters Towers	64m 30s	SUTTON_P01-001911B
Ranji Pope	1970	Charters Towers	62m 40s	SUTTON_P01-001912A
Harry Bunn	1974	Townsville	48m 40s	TSUNODA_T08-003412B
George Reid	1970	Charters Towers	60m 5s	BREEN_G13-001889B

Notes:

While the recordings of Alf Palmer in TSUNODA_T06 to TSUNODA_T09 are given the name of 'Kurijal' they are, in fact, Warrongo.

The recording of George Reid lasts approximately 13 minutes, beginning about 39 minutes into the archived audio file.

The audio recorded for this book has been archived at the Pacific and Regional Archive for Digital Sources in Endangered Cultures. To access, you will first need to sign up as a user at https://catalog.paradisec.org.au/users/sign_up. You can then download it from https://catalog.paradisec.org.au/collections/Yaru.

www.ingramcontent.com/pod-product-compliance
Lightning Source LLC
LaVergne TN
LVHW061048110826
845155LV00033B/32

* 9 7 8 1 9 2 2 1 0 2 4 4 7 *